BURIED BOSTON

AMERICA'S REVOLUTIONARY NECROPOLIS

JR PEPPER

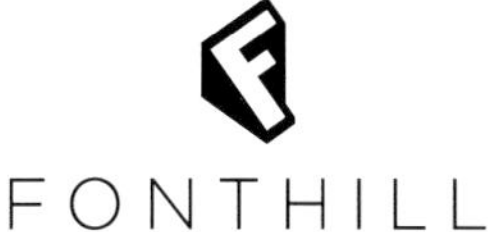
FONTHILL

Fonthill Media Inc.
www.fonthillmedia.com
office@fonthillmedia.com

First published 2024

ISBN 978-1-62545-132-3

Typeset in 10pt on 13pt Sabon
Printed and bound in England

FOREWORD

As someone who works with historic postmortem and bereavement photography, I believe that JR Pepper captures the spirit of cemeteries, turning them into contemplative sanctuaries where the past and the present converge. In doing so, she has created a work of art that is both haunting and inspiring. Her work transcends the notion of a cemetery as a final resting place and transforms it into a "Revolutionary Necropolis," a place where history, art, and the human experience converge in breathtaking and thought-provoking ways.

The lens of a camera has the power to eclipse time, offering us a glimpse of eternity. Pepper's work is a reflection of that power—a reminder that photography is not solely a tool for capturing the present, but also a vessel for bridging the gap between the temporal and the eternal. Her photographs are windows to moments long past, evoking a profound sense of connection to those who have come before us, imploring us to ponder the depth of human existence and the indelible marks we leave on the world. Through Pepper's lens, these monuments are immortalized, preserving the delicate engravings, the fading epitaphs, and the intricate artwork that might otherwise succumb to nature.

Buried Boston: America's Revolutionary Necropolis is more than just an assemblage of stunning photographs. It invites us to contemplate the human condition, our shared mortality, and the enduring power of remembrance. Pepper's keen eye and deep reverence for these sacred spaces encourage us to embrace the past and honor the present. *Buried Boston* is a testament to the enduring power of art to illuminate the hidden corners of our world and reveal the profound beauty that exists in even the most unexpected places.

Elizabeth A. Burns

About the Author

Photographer, lecturer, and self-described "professional eccentric"— JR Pepper has dedicated her life and her studies to the forgotten aspects of art and history. Pepper is recognized for her work in spirit photography which has been featured on Vice.com, *Musee Magazine*, and Dave Thompson's *Haunted America FAQ*. With over twenty years of experience in photography and image retouching, she has worked on numerous publications and projects with various archives and museums. She regularly lectures with *The Brooklyn Brainery*, *The Dead Ladies Show*, is a fellow with the Odd Salon, and past lecturer with *Atlas Obscura*. She proudly works as an assistant and digital imaging specialist to Dr. Stanley Burns and Liz Burns of The Burns Archive, adjunct professor at Brooklyn College, and taphophile tour guide at Green-Wood Cemetery. She lives in Brooklyn with two guinea pigs, her spaniel mix, Lydia, and too many books.

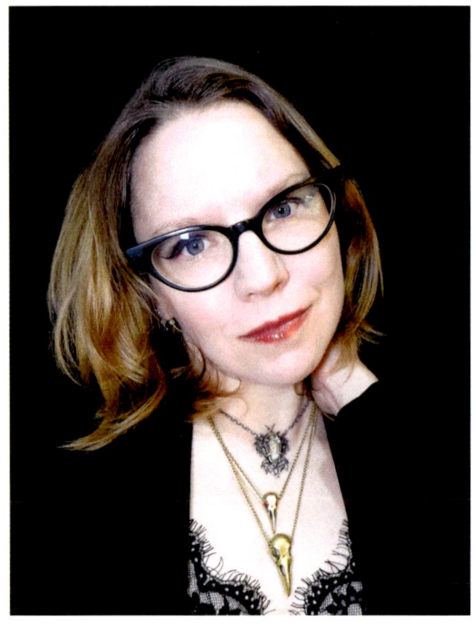

Photograph by JR Pepper.

Contents

Foreword 3

About the Author 4

Acknowledgments 6

Introduction 7

1 King's Chapel Burying Ground, Established 1630 9

2 Eliot Burying Ground, Established 1630 17

3 Phipps Street Burying Ground, Established 1630 31

4 Copp's Hill Burying Ground, Established 1659 38

5 Granary Burying Ground, Established 1660 47

6 Central Burying Ground, Established 1756 61

7 Mount Auburn Cemetery, Established 1831 69

8 Forest Hills Cemetery, Established 1848 79

9 St. Michael's Cemetery, Established 1907 87

Endnotes 92

Bibliography 95

Acknowledgments

I have been blessed enough to have family and friends who have taken my macabre, taphophile interest with a willing smile. To those that have wandered a new cemetery trail with me, coffee in hand, and listened to me ramble on about mausoleum architecture or cemetery parrots—this book could not have happened without you. To my regular cemetery travelers my sincerest thanks—but especially Cassy, Cook, Lucas, Marsha, Zev, Katie, Lailah, Lucey and Richard—thank you for your patience as I dragged you through many a necropolis on our vacations and meandering walks home. This book would not have been possible without my friend and colleague, Allison C. Meier, who remains my constant teacher. Increasing thanks are also due to N.M. Scuri for their diligent editing. I also send my warmest thanks to The Burns Archive and all my "church-going" friends from my veterinary family for their constant warmth and friendship.

Most importantly, thanks to my family but most especially my father, Robert, for his constant support and encouragement of his strange and unusual daughter.

INTRODUCTION

It's no surprise why I am enamored with cemeteries. When I was growing up, I was bewildered by the tale of *Sleepy Hollow*, rewatching the animated movie more times than my poor parents could stand. To bring the matter closer to home, my father grew up across the street from Brooklyn's own Green-Wood Cemetery. He would tell me stories of him and his friends playing tag and leaping across gravestones as a boy. It may come as no surprise, but I have been happily drawn to them. That wasn't always the case.

I remember staying at my grandmother's home across from the cemetery. No matter what I did, I couldn't fall asleep. I stared out the window for hours watching the light dance across the tombstones, terrified. The next morning, when my grandmother asked me if I had been afraid to fall asleep, all I could do with my exhausted nine-year-old head was nod.

Grandma Mary just shook her head and said that when I grew up that I would learn that it's the things *outside* of the cemetery that you should be afraid of. Years later, when the pandemic caused the world to shut down, cemeteries became a rare sense of comfort, a means to escape the troubled city.

It seems my grandmother knew what she was talking about after all.

Cemeteries are giant outdoor museums, each with a hidden history, but only if you know where to look. I've made it my life's work to explore and document these sculpture gardens filled with memories, hope, and a sense of solace. No trip is ever complete without wandering through a cemetery, camera in hand, and a chance to chronicle lifetimes long past.

This book is just one of many cemetery-based adventures that I have been lucky enough to explore. Boston has some of the oldest burying grounds in the United States, with over sixteen scattered throughout the city. They aren't terribly difficult to find either; a quick walk away from Back Bay station will find you on Boston's historic Freedom Trail. This nearly 2.5-mile path throughout the meandering streets of Boston explores various historic sites, including numerous burying grounds.

In addition to being home to dozens of traditional burying grounds, just outside of Boston, in Cambridge, Massachusetts, is the stunningly beautiful Mount Auburn

Cemetery. Mount Auburn is America's first rural cemetery. Rural cemeteries, or garden cemeteries as they are often called, are known for their rich green landscapes, opulent monuments, and massive mausoleums. Cemeteries like Mount Auburn offered a beautiful respite from the crowded cities and churchyard burial grounds. They also demonstrate the dynamic shifting attitudes towards death in the nineteenth century. These cemeteries were filled with a set of symbolic imagery all their own. They were no longer filled with death's heads and warnings of *memento mori*, "remember that you must die." Instead, they were filled with statues of angels, stone flowers, and sentiments of hopefulness and the possibility that death is not the end.

The cemeteries and burying grounds of Boston reveal the city's rich history, demonstrate a shift in funeral trends, and memorialize the dead—all while revealing a unique story slumbering among the gravestones. The word cemetery comes from the Greek for "sleeping place," after all.

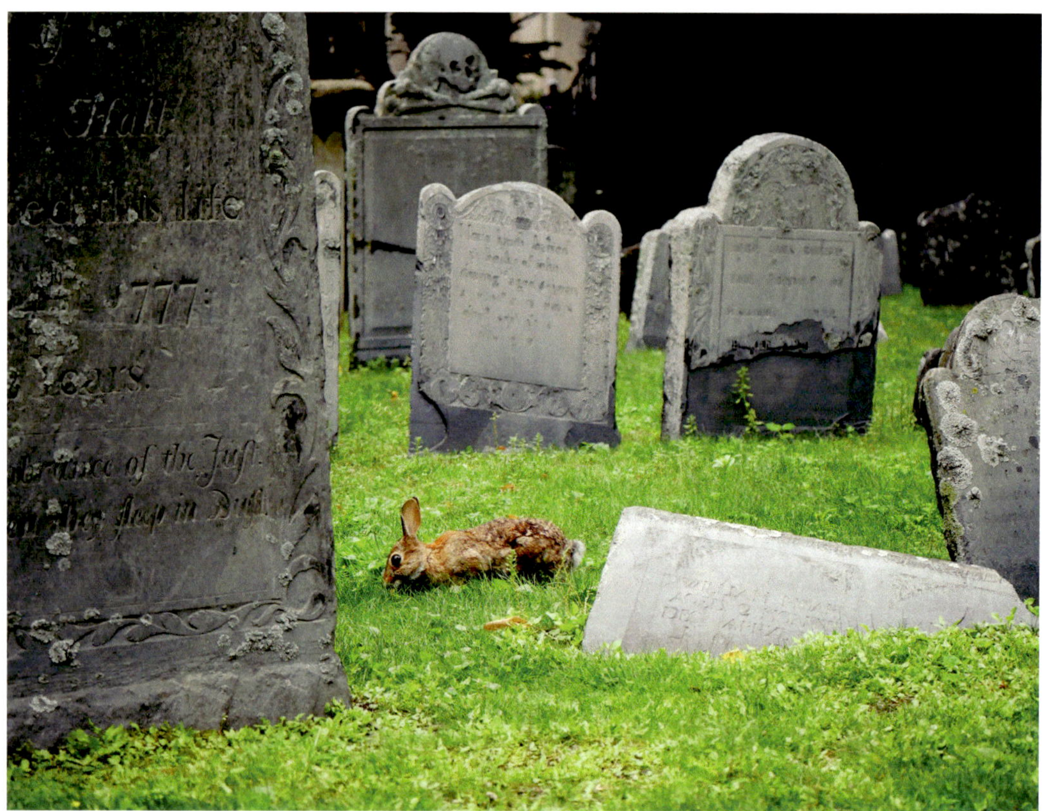

One of the many fluffy residents of Boston's burying grounds.

1

King's Chapel Burying Ground

Located on Tremont Street, King's Chapel Burying Ground is reportedly the oldest burying ground in Boston.[1] King's Chapel is a well-organized collection of over 500 headstones in neatly organized rows and holds the remains of more than 1,000 people.

Upon entering the grounds, you are greeted by the curvaceous stone dedicated to Joseph Tapping. Tapping's monument has two distinctly separate narratives. The top part of the tombstone has a winged death's head flanked by ornate leaves and spirals.[2] An hourglass, a symbol of time's rapid passing, can be seen just above the death's head—an apt symbol considering Tapping died in his twenties. Directly underneath is an intricate portrayal of the struggle between life and death. Depicted as an immense skeleton, Death is attempting to extinguish the candle of life with a candle snuffer. To the right, Father Time feebly attempts to stay Death's cadaverous hand. The unique design of Tapping's stone is credited to the Old Stone Cutter, also known as the Charlestown Stone Cutter, and the Stone Cutter of Boston. Although there are multiple tombstones in Boston featuring the Stonecutter's distinct carvings, the artisan's true identity remains a secret to this day.

A second and equally macabre tombstone within King's Chapel attributed to the Old Stone Cutter is dedicated to Mehetabel Sheafe, who died at only a few months old. On Mehetabel's stone is a large skeleton, with a small person clearly seen trapped within its sizeable rib cage. The immediate assumption is that this image suggests perhaps an unborn child. However, this striking visual shows man as death's eternal prisoner. The image might seem curious, but it is likely taken from Francis Quarles' popular book, *Emblems and Hieroglyphics of the Life of Man*, published in 1683.[3] The book contains numerous bizarre and allegorical illustrations often accompanied with prose and scripture.

These remarkable and detailed carvings mark a definitive shift away from the more traditional Puritan stones which would feature a mere epitaph. The work of the Old Stone Cutter adds specific personal touches and an individual style that may very well have been an inspiration for the personalized tombstones during the Victorian era.

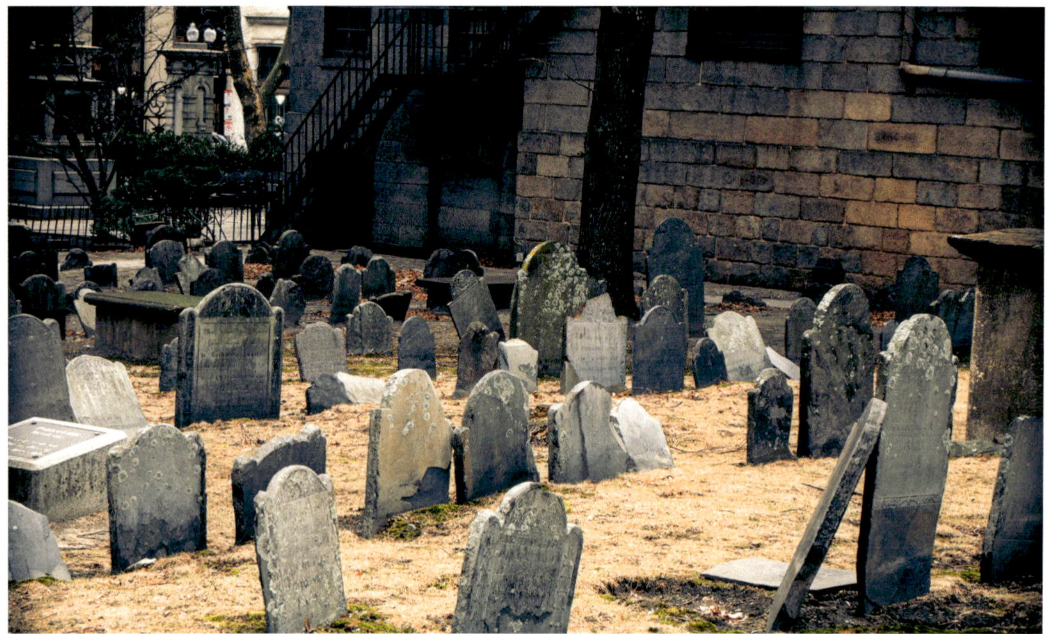

King's Chapel Burying Ground on a cold winter afternoon.

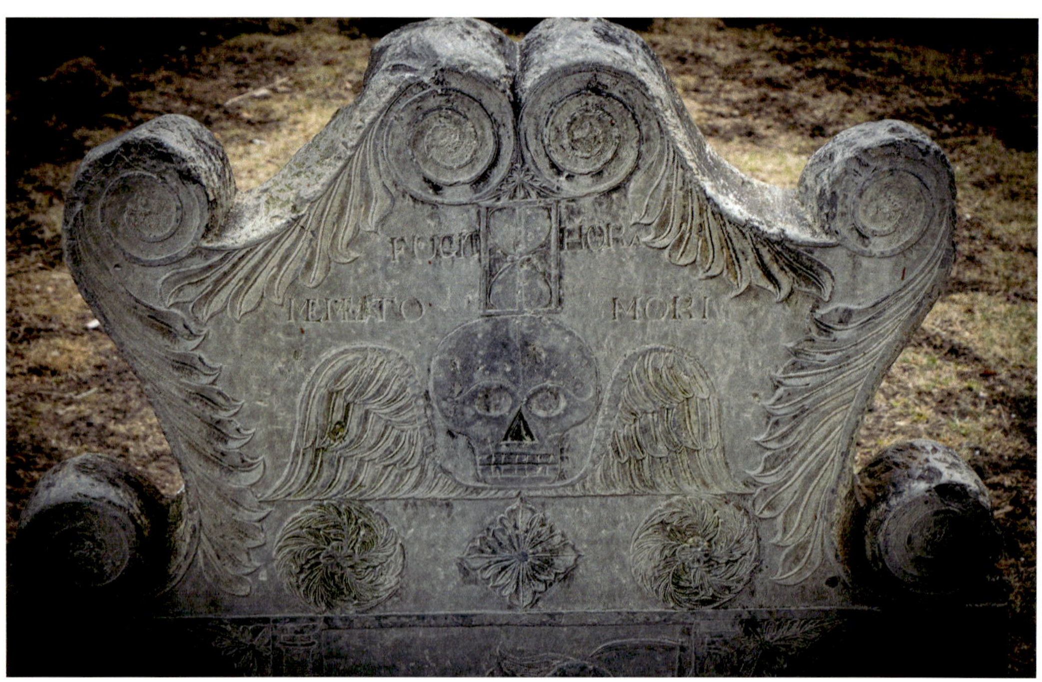

The grave of Joseph Tapping features an elaborate design by the Old Stone Cutter, also known as the Boston Stone Cutter. Next to the hourglass of Life reads the Latin phrases, *Fugit hora,* "time flies"; and *memento mori*, "Remember that you will die."

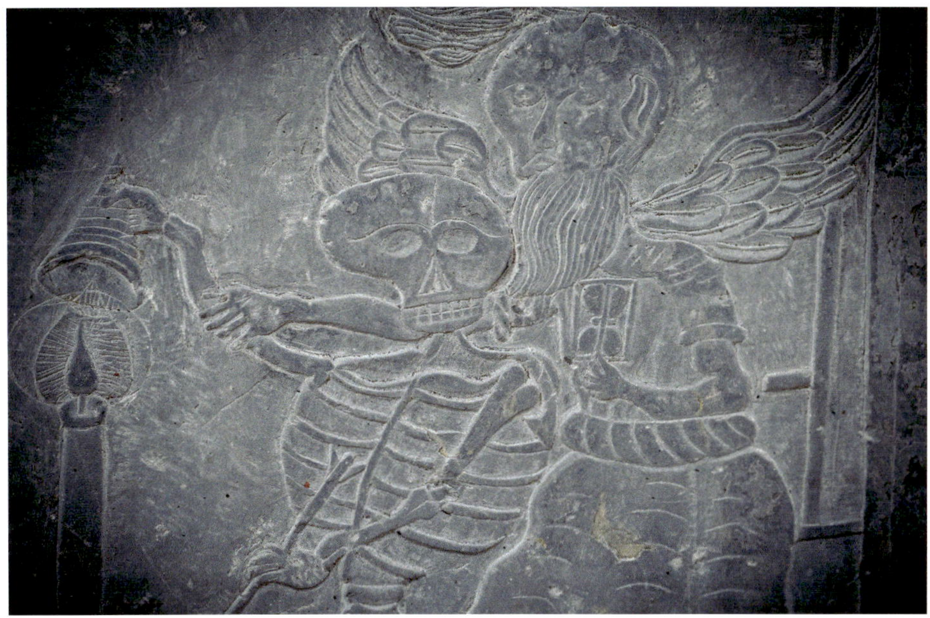

Father Time as he tries to stay the hand of Death from extinguishing the candle of Life. A nearby Latin inscription reads *Tempus edit*, "Time will come."

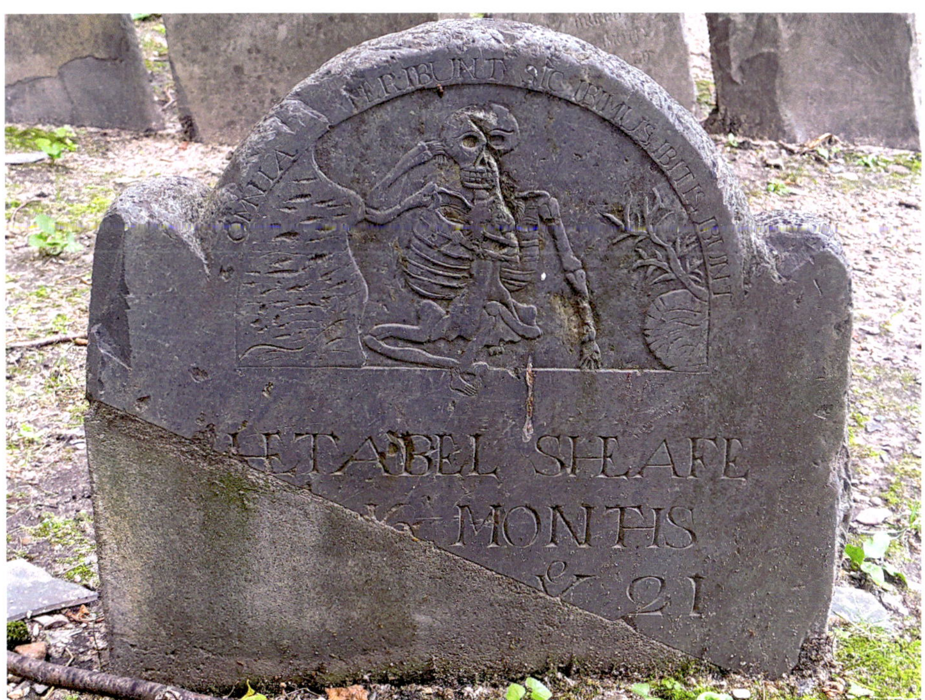

Blink and you'll miss the remarkable stone for Mehetabel Sheafe, with man as the prisoner of death.

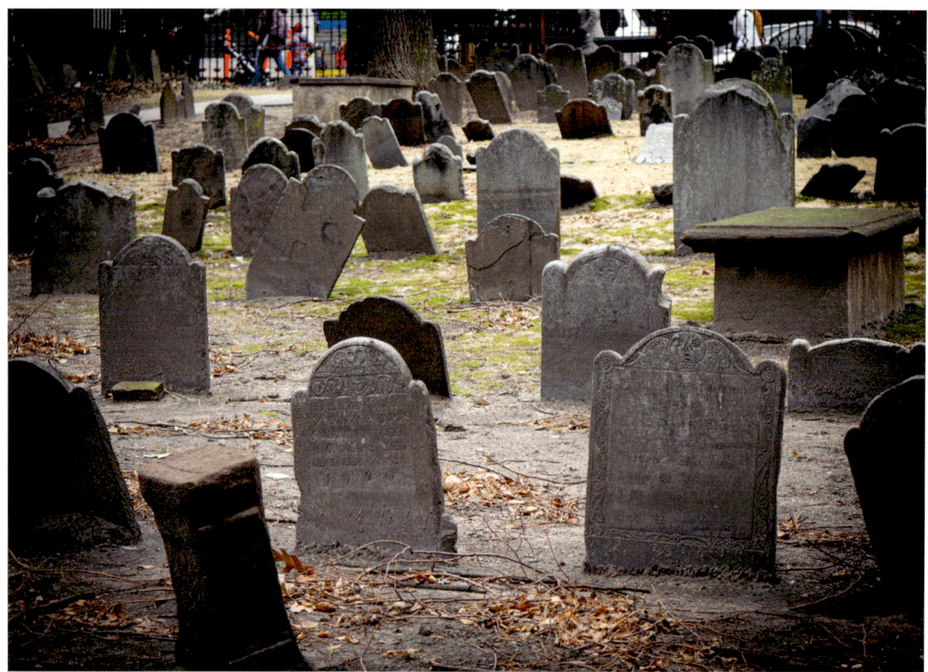

King's Chapel Burying Ground is hidden between dozens of shops and restaurants.

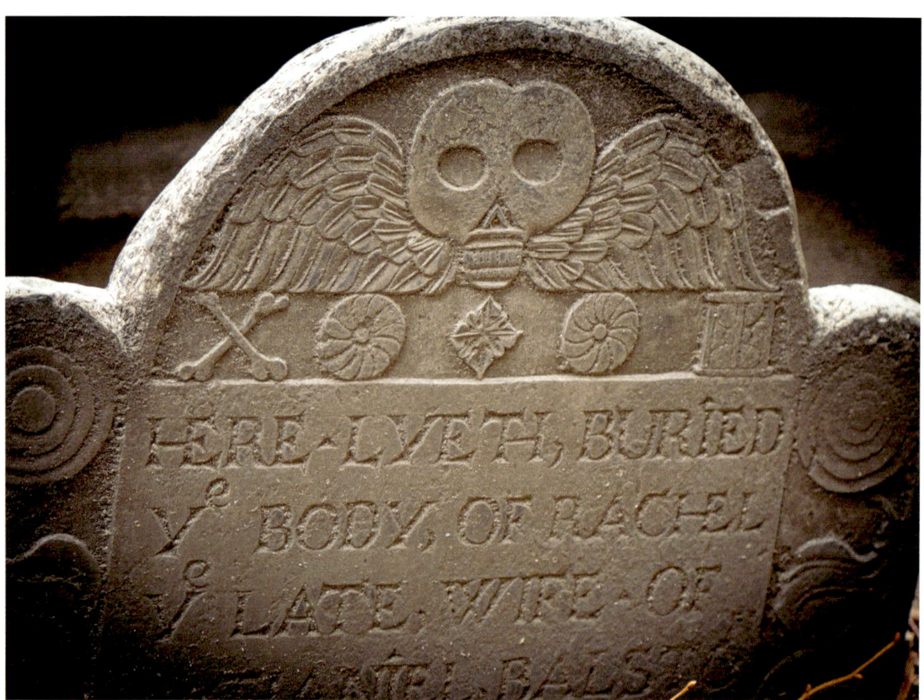

One of the death's head markers at King's Chapel.

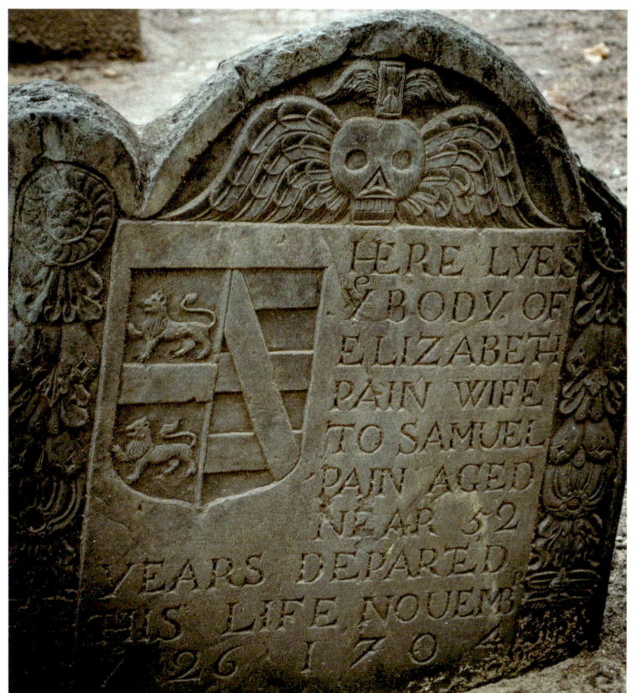

Right: The memorial dedicated to Elizabeth Pain, Samuel Pain's wife, features not one, but two *memento mori* symbols, along with a family crest.

Below: The death's head motif is shown in a variety of ways, such as this one with a *fleur-de-lis*.

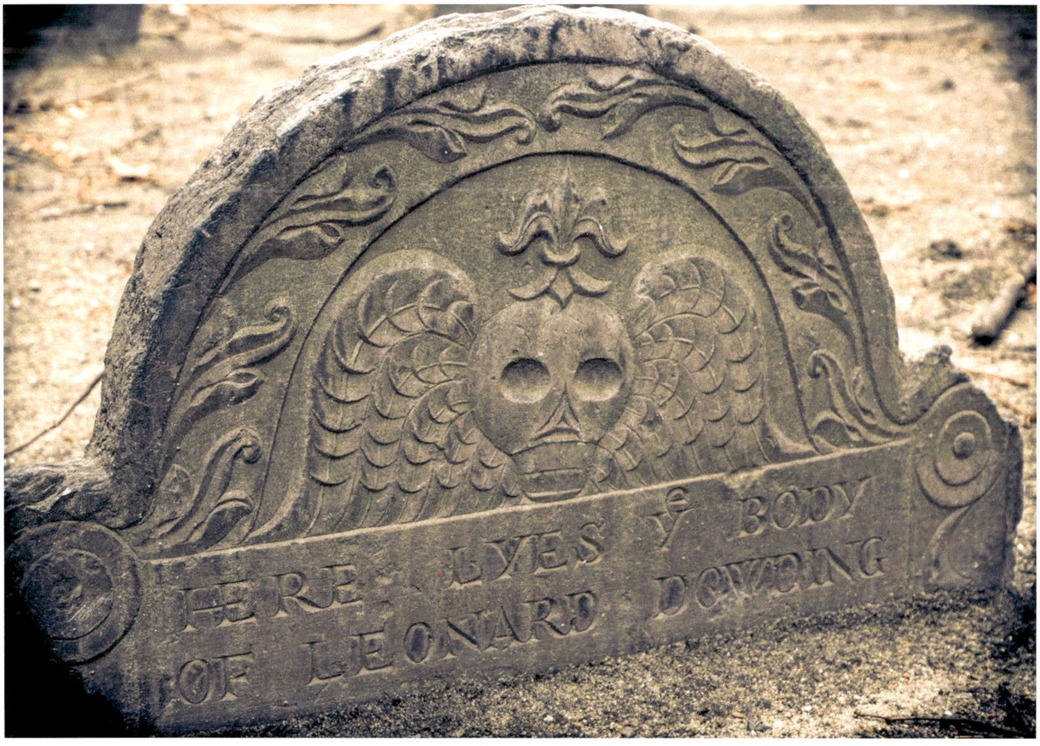

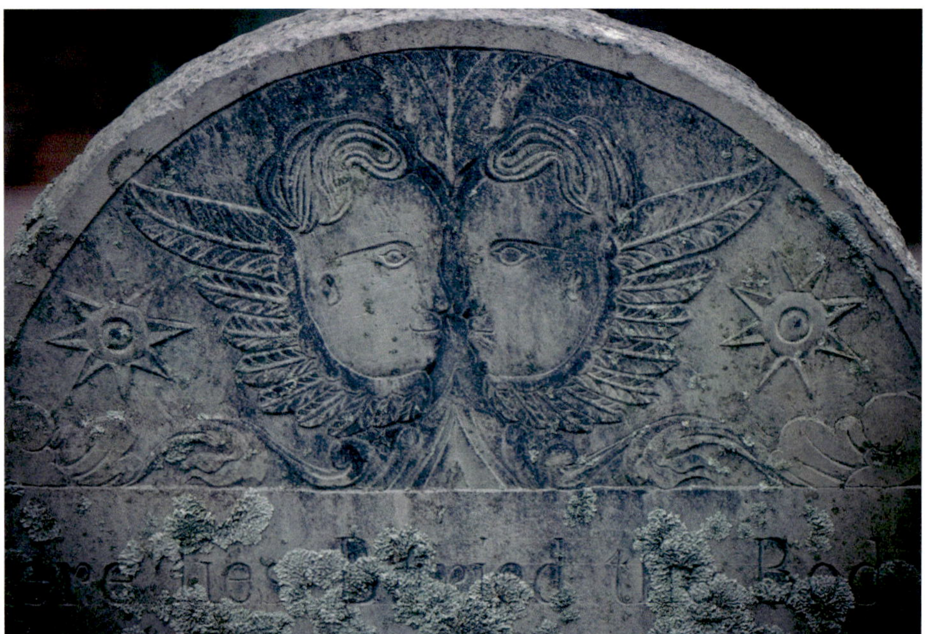

Epitaph featuring two cherub heads and a solar motif.

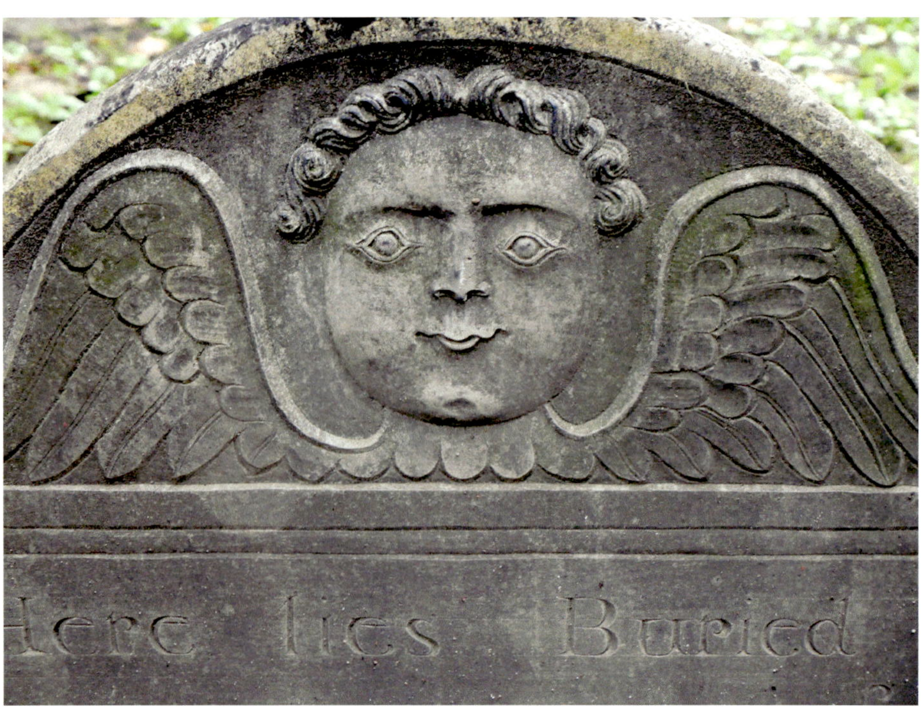

Some of the memorials have a variety of elaborate details, like this one with elaborately curled hair and a quivering lip.

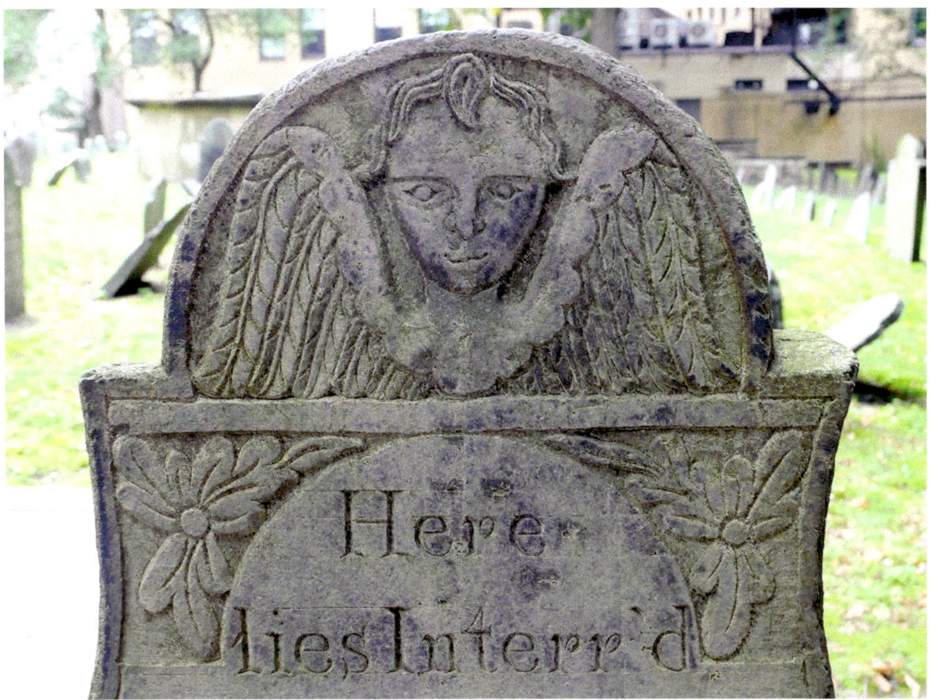

The stone dedicated to Mrs. Elizabeth Foster, died sixty-one, featuring a face with a dominant curl in front of their head.

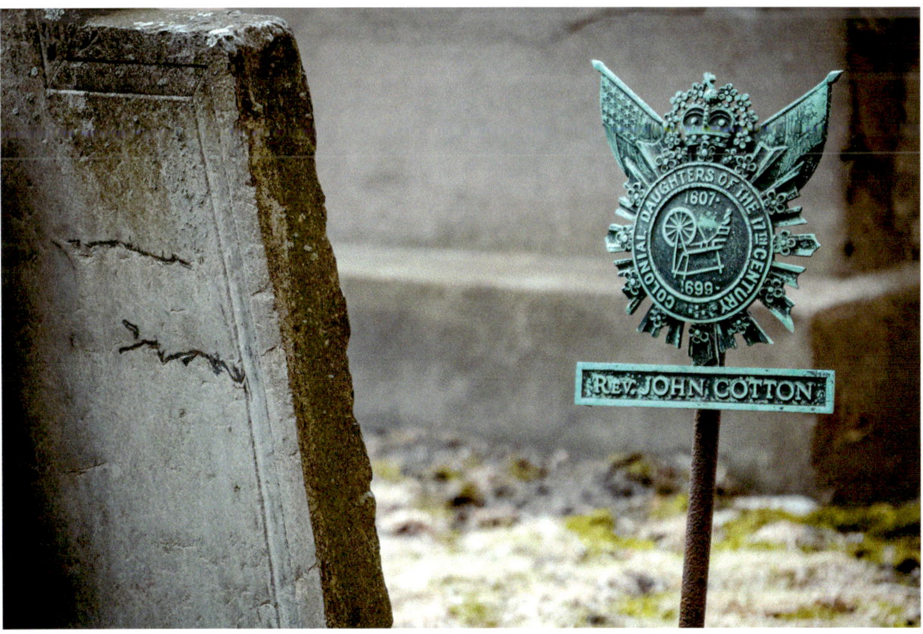

Metal sign designating the grave of Reverend John Cotton.

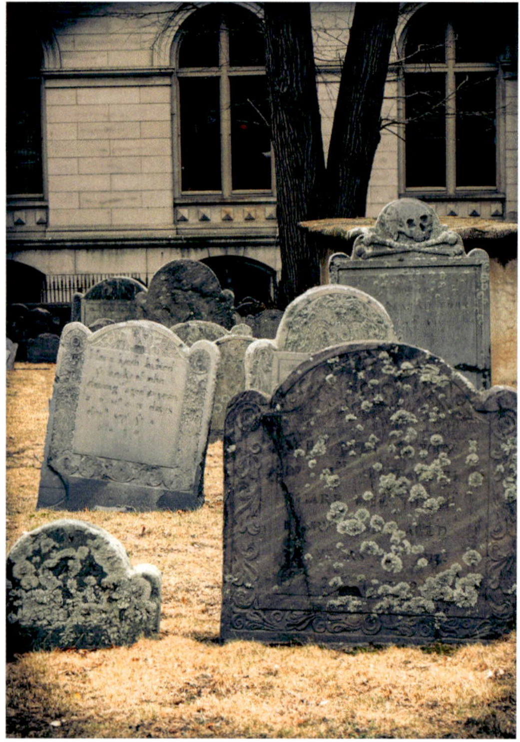

Many of the stones at King's Chapel Burying Ground have shifted over time, or are covered densely with lichens.

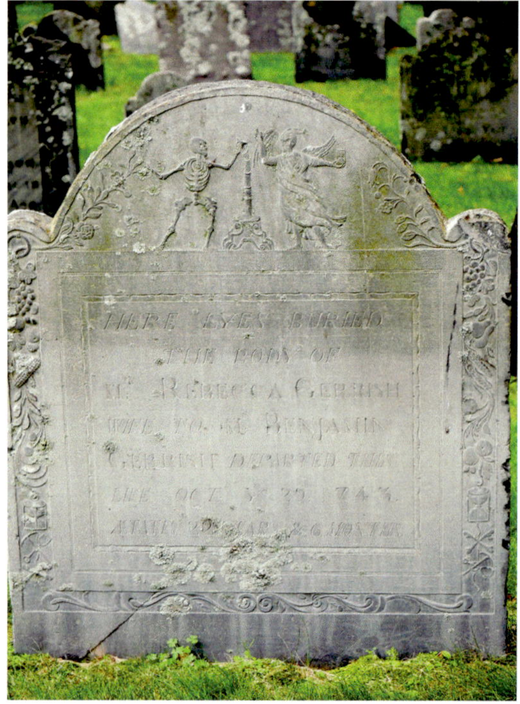

The tombstone to Rebecca Gerrish shows a battle between Father Time and Death; note the hourglass in the hand of Father Time.

2

Eliot Burying Ground

Originally known as the First Burying Ground in Roxbury or the Eustis Street Burying Ground, Eliot Burying Ground had its first burial as far back as 1633. The burial ground is one of the oldest in Boston and is named for the Christian missionary Rev. John Eliot. The burial ground is also notable for the role it played when Boston was under siege in the Revolutionary War. The colonists defended the road to Roxbury at this location and it became known as the Burying Ground Redoubt.

The Eliot Burying Ground is fairly small compared to the mammoth rural cemeteries of Massachusetts. However, there are more graves here than the visible stones indicate. Records for this graveyard do not mention, or even note, the names or sites for an unknown number of enslaved people buried; however, according to Kelly Thomas, Director of Boston's Historic Burying Grounds Initiative, they are interred everywhere within the grounds.[1]

The burying grounds are surrounded by a high stone wall and metal fence. Additional precautions have also been taken, as the grounds can only be accessed by a key and password that must be requested in advance. While this is an effort to discourage vandalism, it also makes the burying ground a personal experience for today's modern taphophile traveler. The Eliot Burying Ground is scarcely acknowledged by the people who live and work here. The living go about their day within the many shops and nearby hospital, all the while being within reach of the oldest burial ground in Roxbury. Recently, an extensive restoration and conservation project repaired over 100 stones.[2]

The memorials here are very much in the style of traditional Puritan symbolism. They remain very minimal, often nothing more than a name, followed by the date of birth and death. In cases where imagery is shown, it is usually in the form of skulls with wings, or crossbones, each a symbol of the inevitability of death. More elaborate ones with engravings of urns, weeping willows, and hourglasses can also be found throughout the grounds.

The earliest grave within Eliot is also one of the earliest in all of Boston. It belongs to Samuel Danforth, who was born and died in 1653, not long after the Puritans settled here. Samuel's marker is small, difficult to read, and nearly entirely obscured by the earth. Samuel is buried with his eight brothers and sisters, many of whom died before adulthood. His father, also named Samuel, is buried not far away, in the nearby Dudley Tomb.[3]

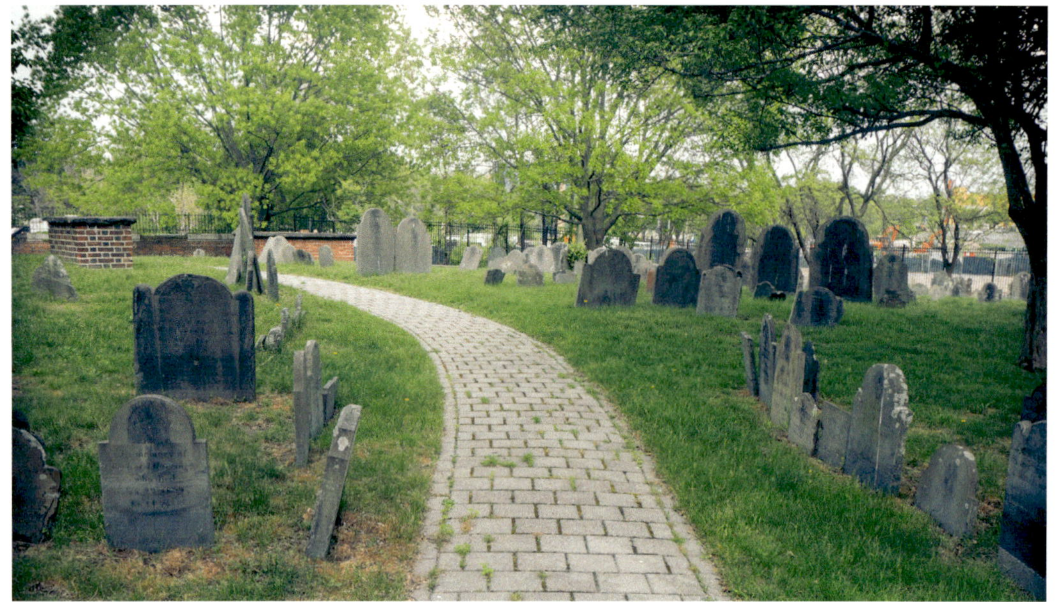

Past a locked gate and up a small staircase is Eliot Burying Ground, formerly known as Eustis Street Burying Ground.

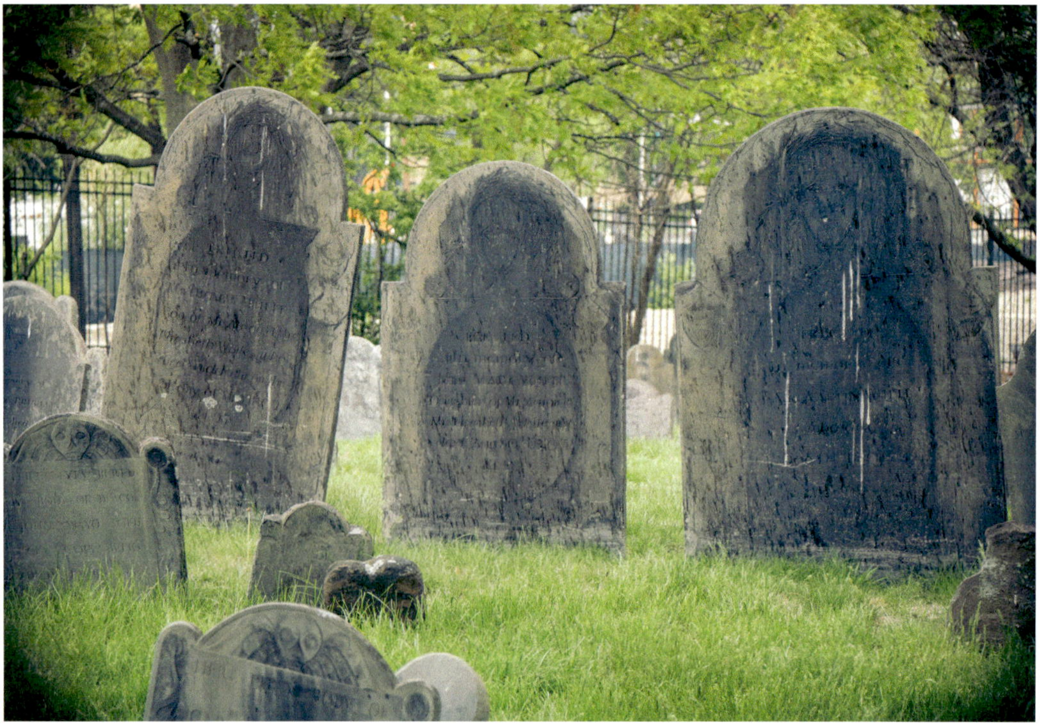

Numerous stones at Eliot Burying Ground feature symbols of urns.

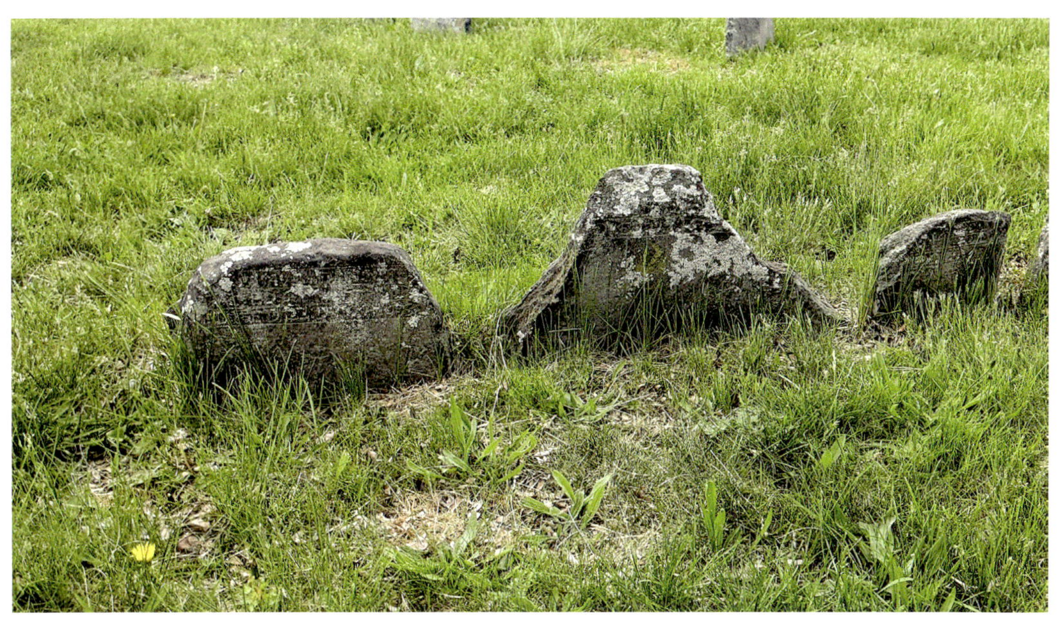

The oldest stone in Eliot, and reportedly the oldest stone in Boston, is dedicated to Samuel Danforth, who died in 1653 at only six months old.

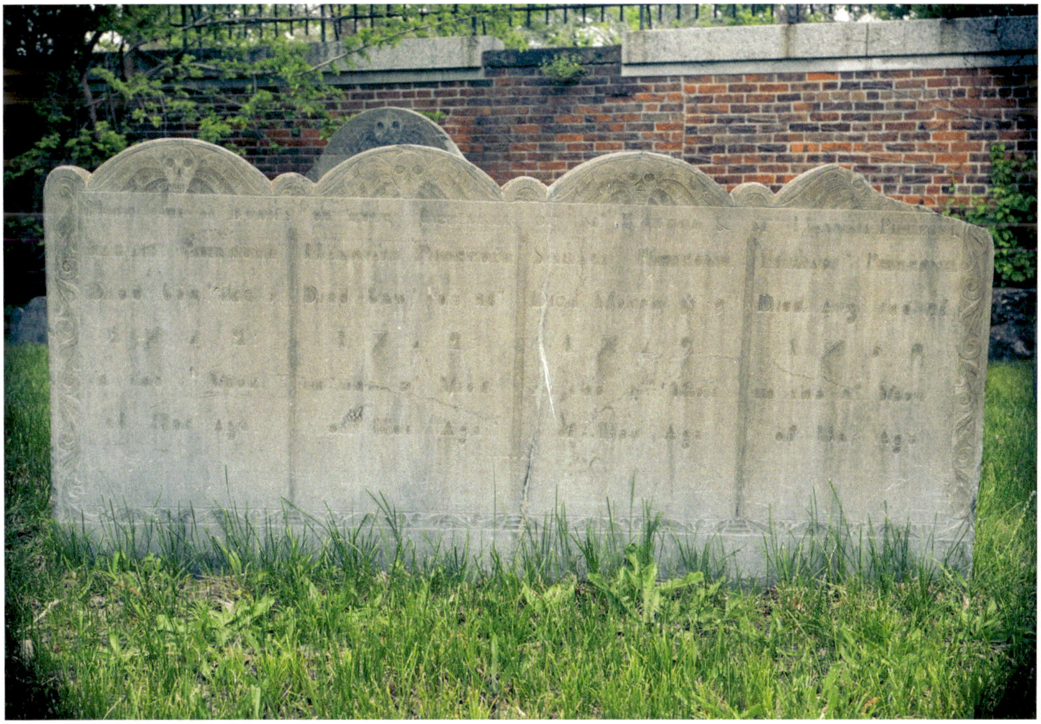

The connected gravestones of the Pierpont family.

A short walk away is one of the largest monuments within Eliot Burying Ground. Four interconnected stones, each with a death's head marker, commemorate the short lives of the Pierpont children, Sarah, Hannah, Sarah, and Elizabeth. Their mother, also named Hannah, is buried nearby, having died the same year as one of her children. Unfortunately, due to the high infant mortality rate and increased rate of infectious disease, similar family mass burials are fairly common.

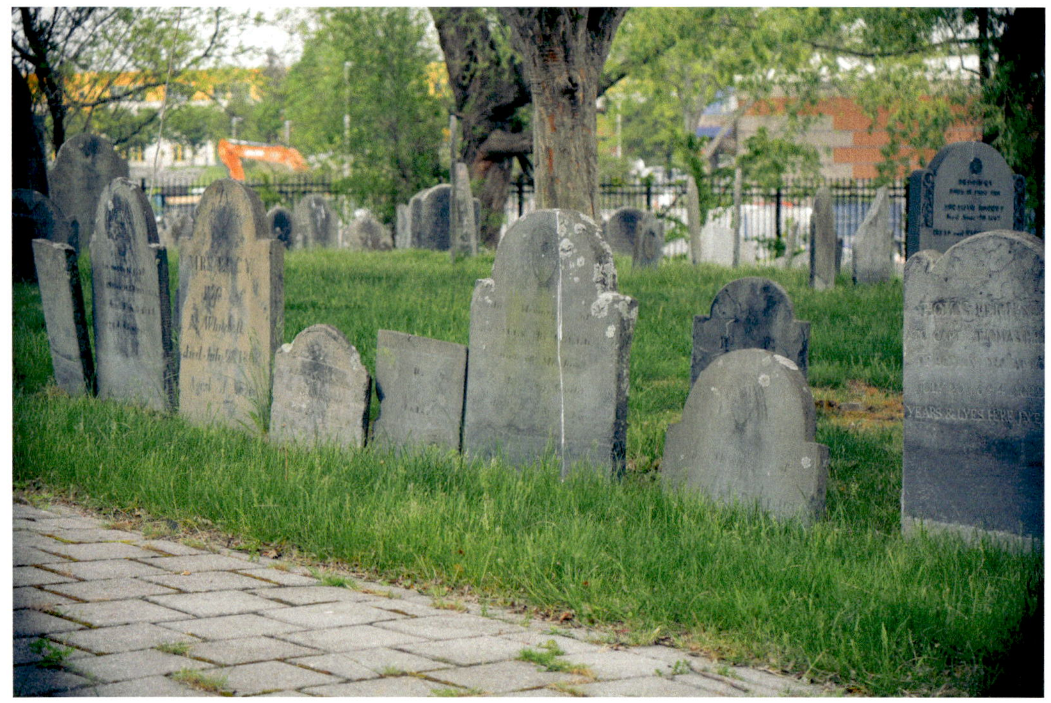

Rows of stones at Eliot Burying Ground.

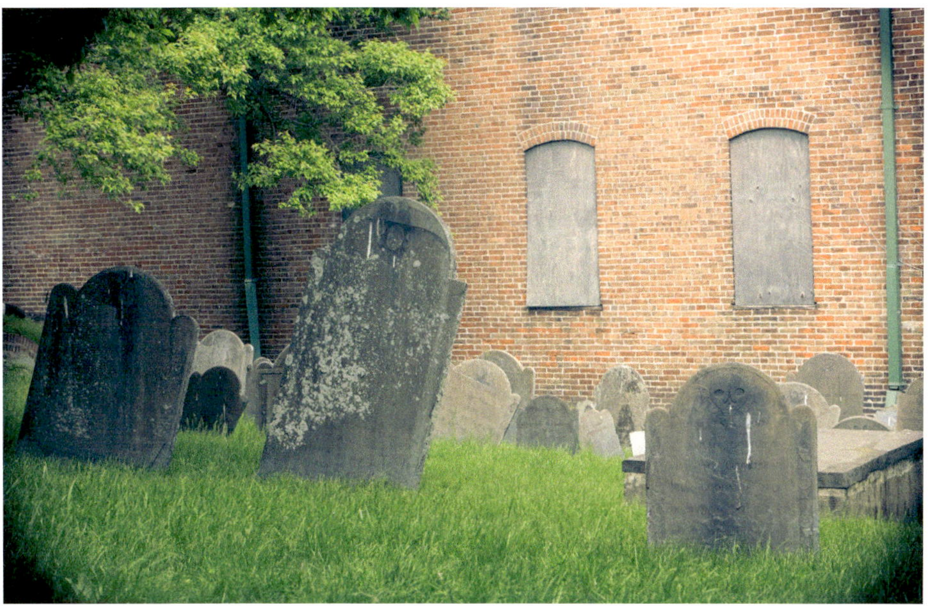

The building behind these stones is obviously a later edition, as the city has sprouted up around the burying ground.

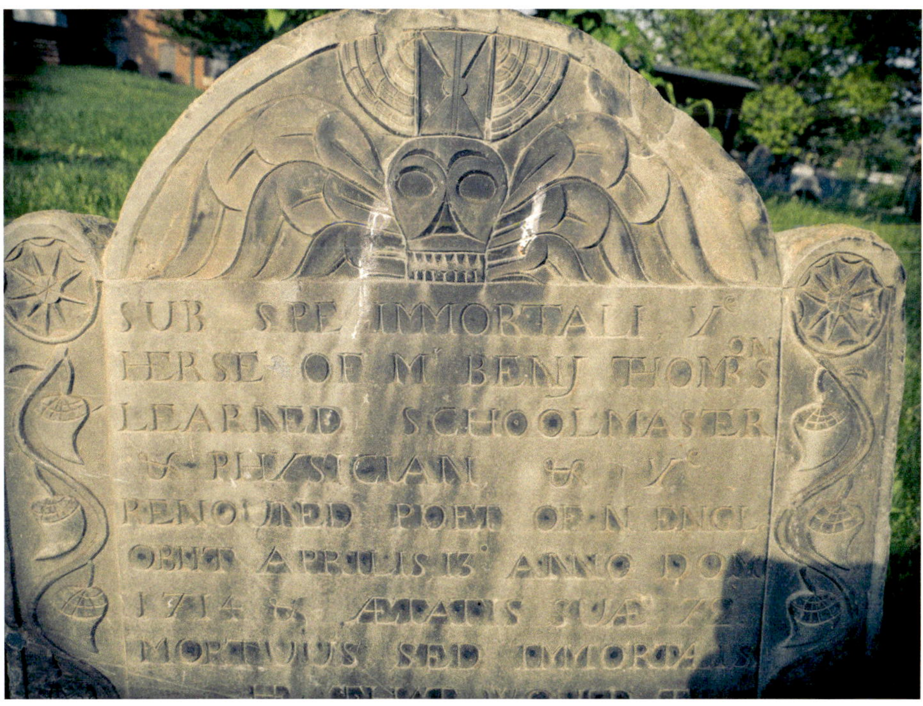

Floral and plant motifs are not uncommon, such as the acorn motif seen on the sides of this monument.

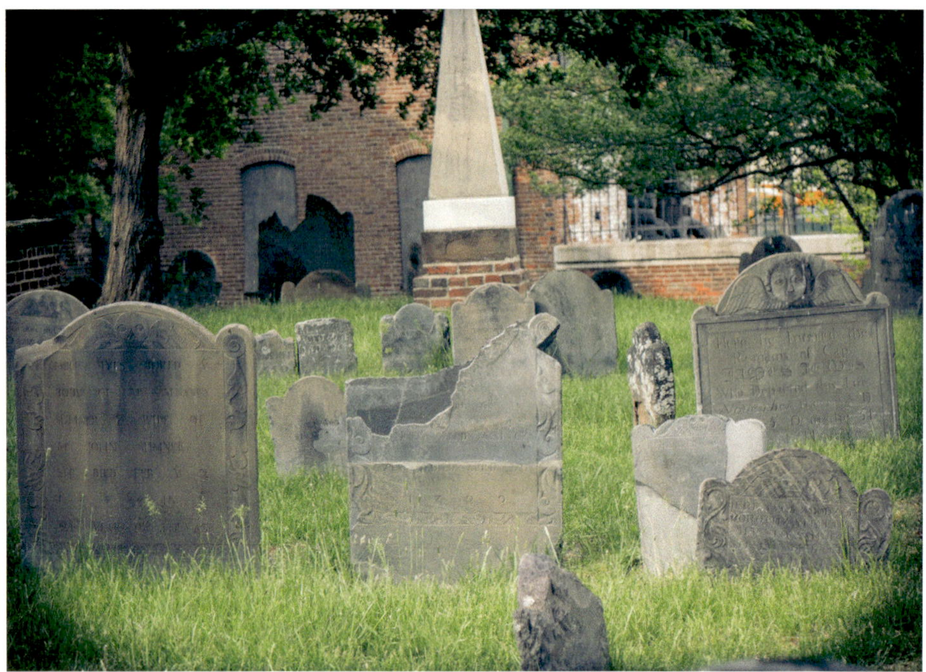

While extensive restoration and conservation efforts have taken place, there are still a number of broken stones.

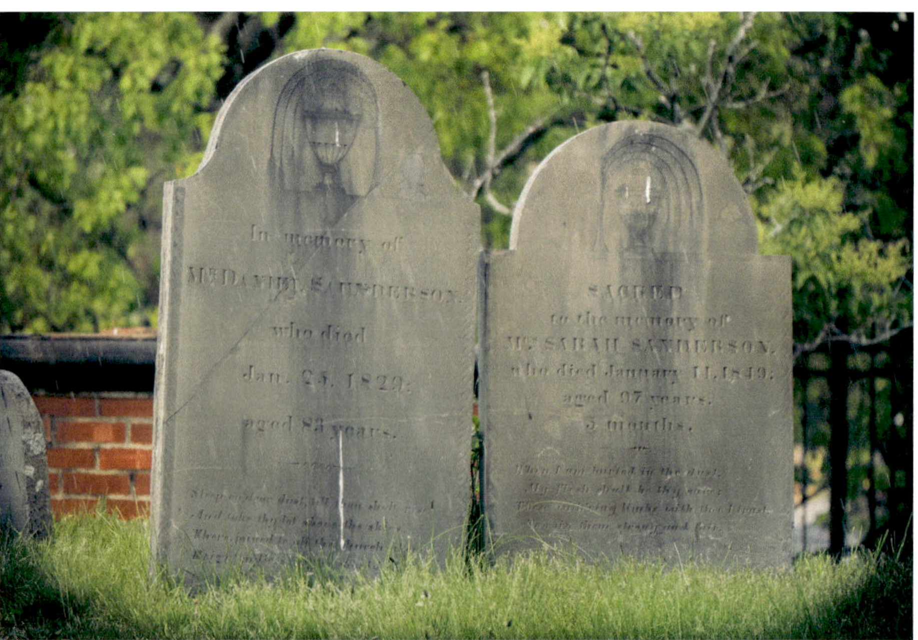

Matching urn symbols are seen on the memorials of Daniel and Sarah Sanderson, both of whom lived to old age.

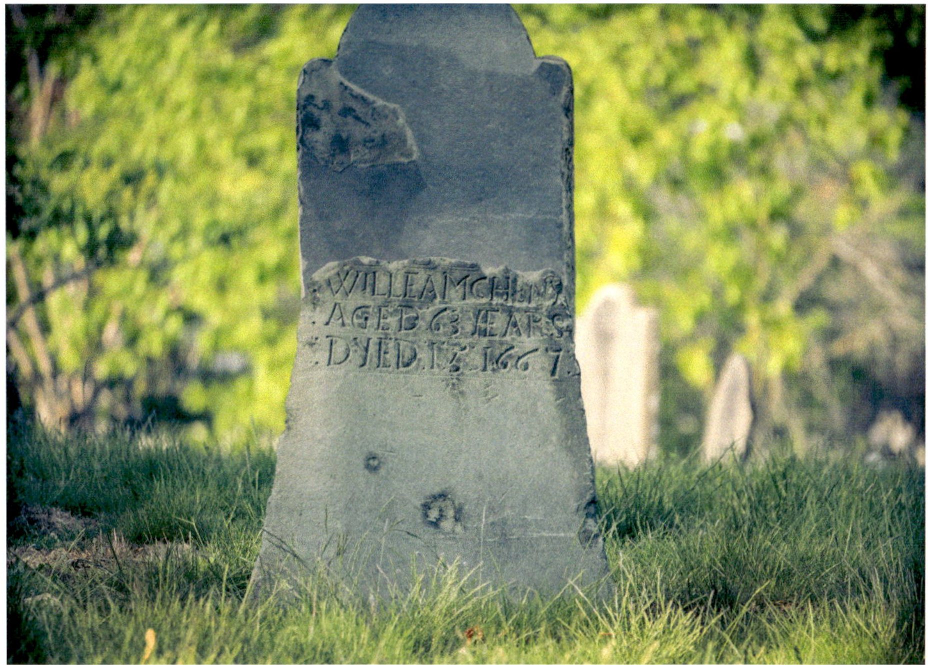

The name of the deceased is difficult to make out; all that remains is the age and date of death.

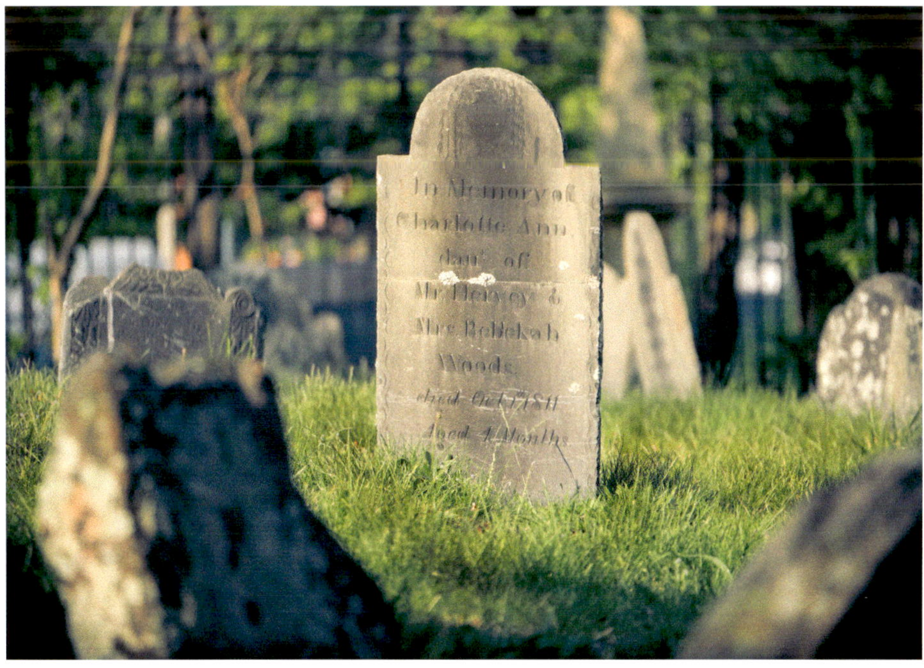

A simple monument dedicated to a young girl, with an urn and willow motif.

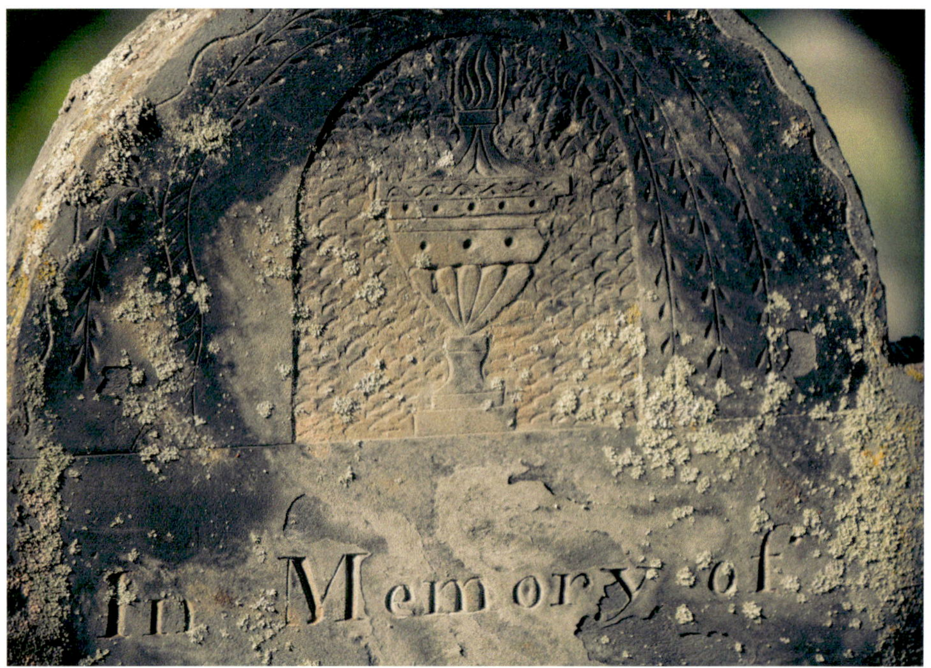

Overgrowth can be seen on many of the stones.

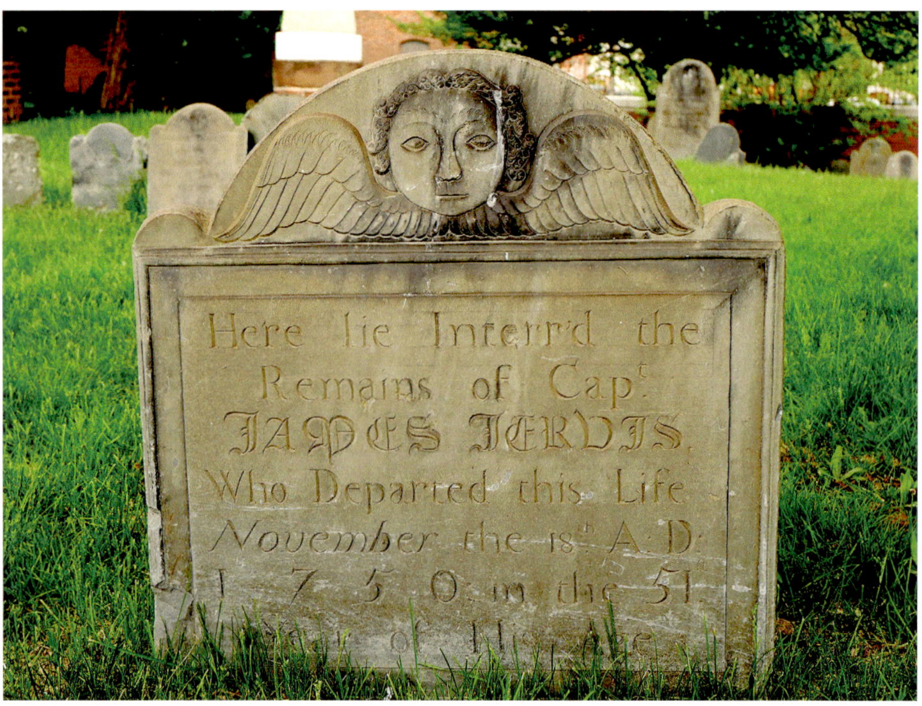

A winged cherub with a curled hair adorns this grave.

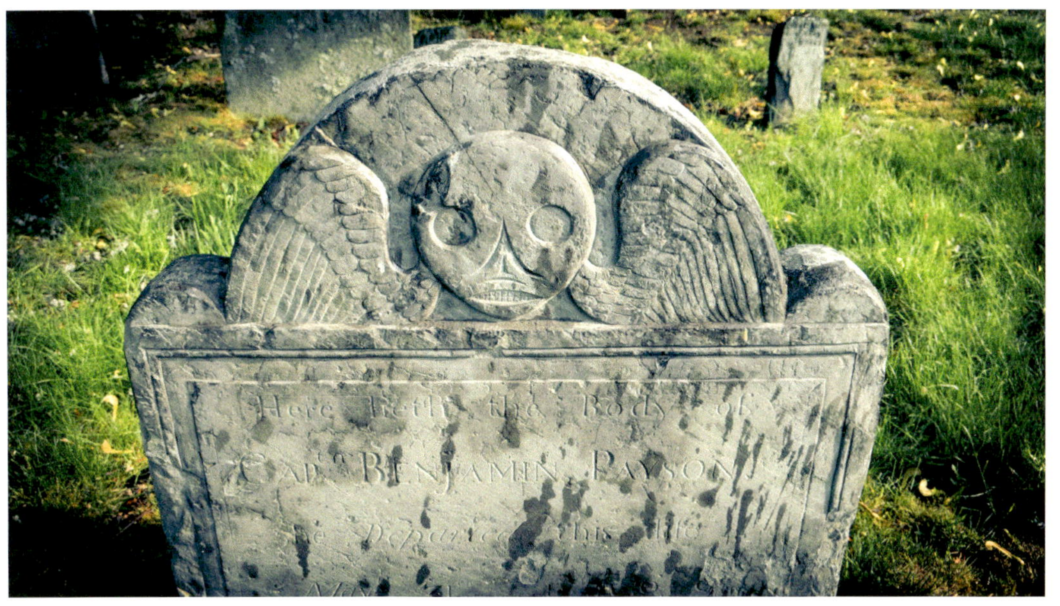

A death's head with exaggerated eyes and grinning skeletal teeth.

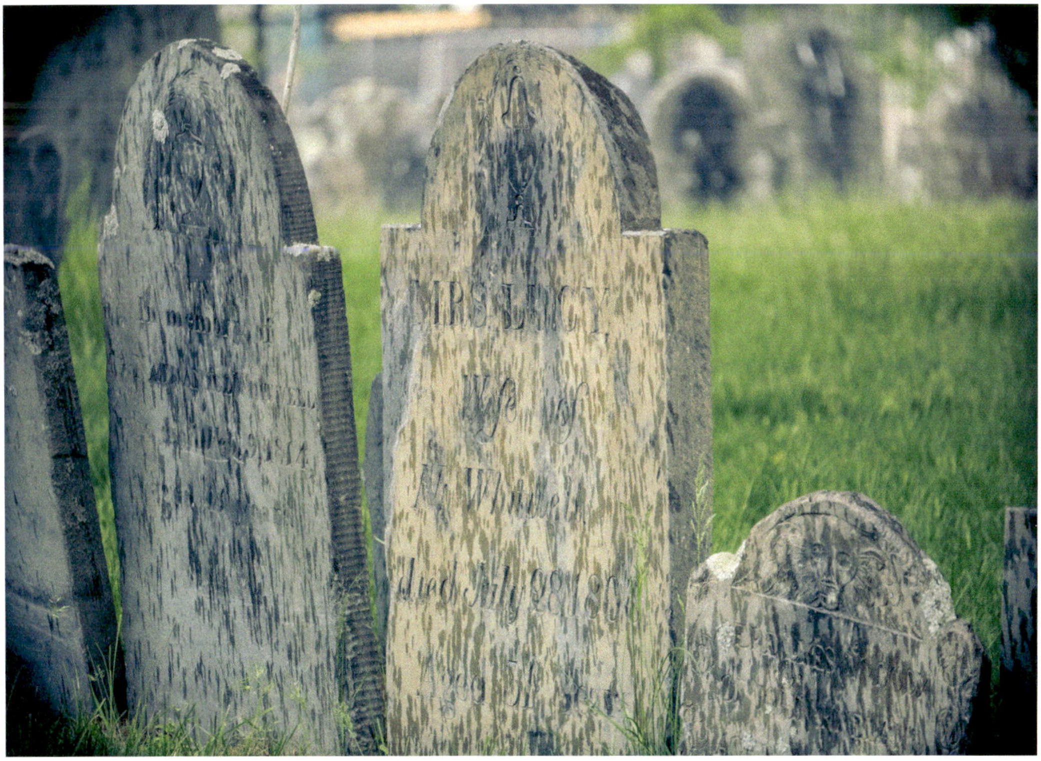

Rain splattered tombstones.

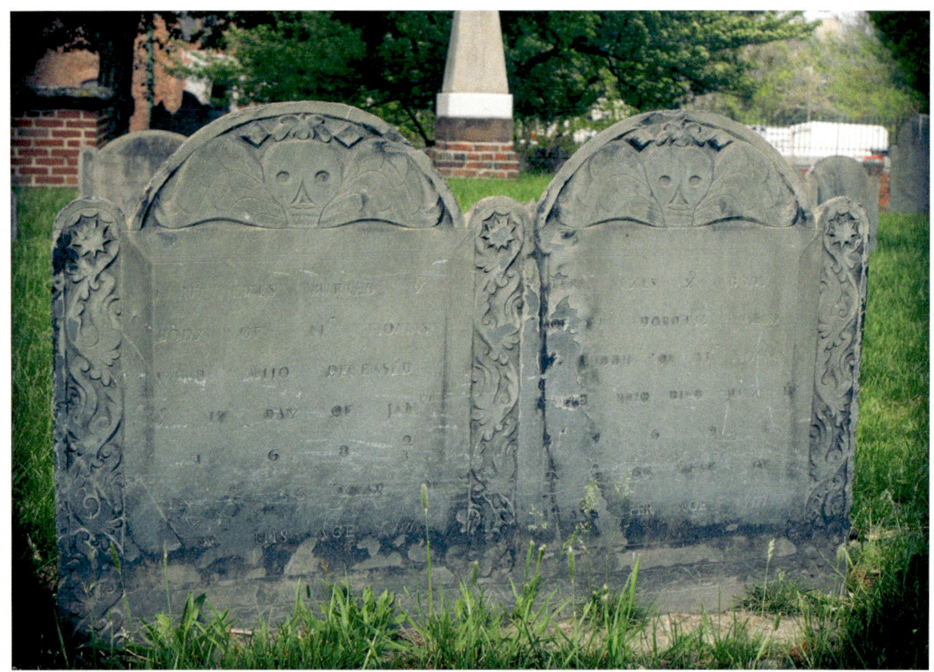

Conjoined tombstones were often used for families and married couples.

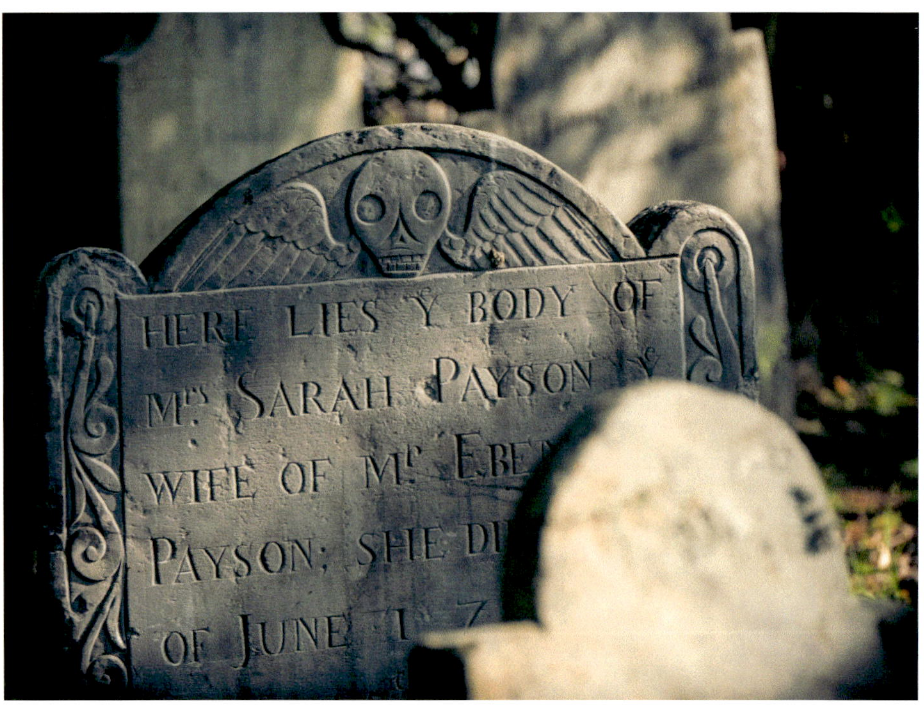

Sunlit tombstone with a death's head motif.

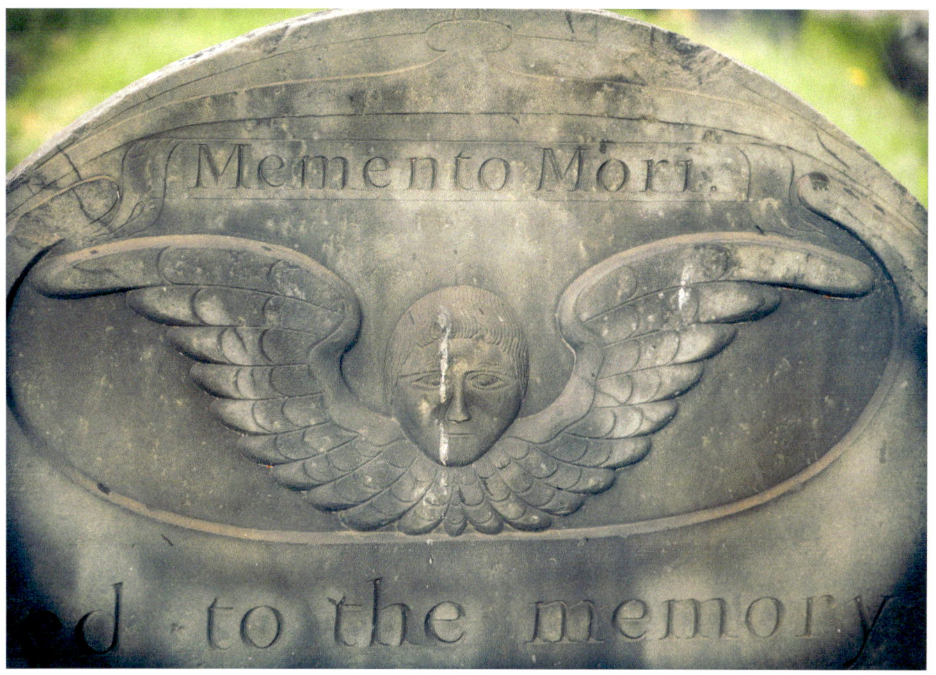

Cherub with loose hair and *memento mori* scroll.

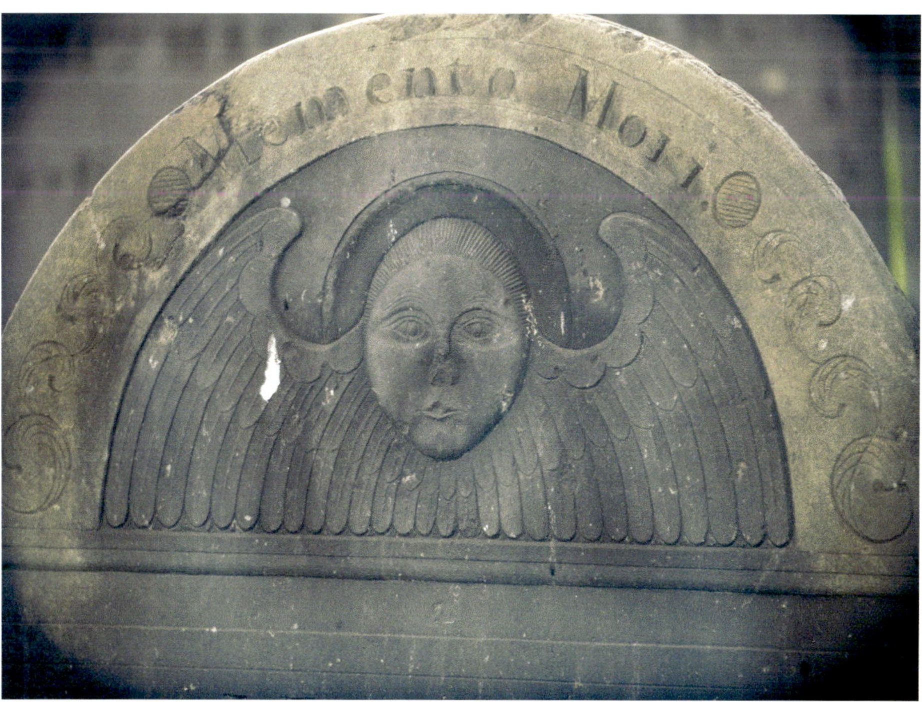

Winged cherub with swept back hair and prominent halo.

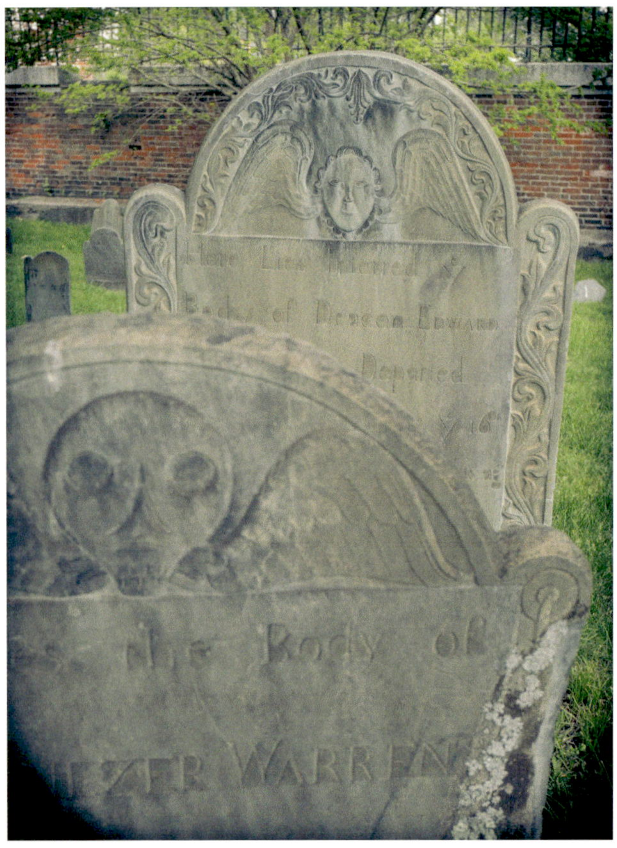

Left: Two of the most frequent symbols seen at Eliot Burying Ground.

Below: A particularly macabre yet atypical sentiment within Boston's many burying grounds.

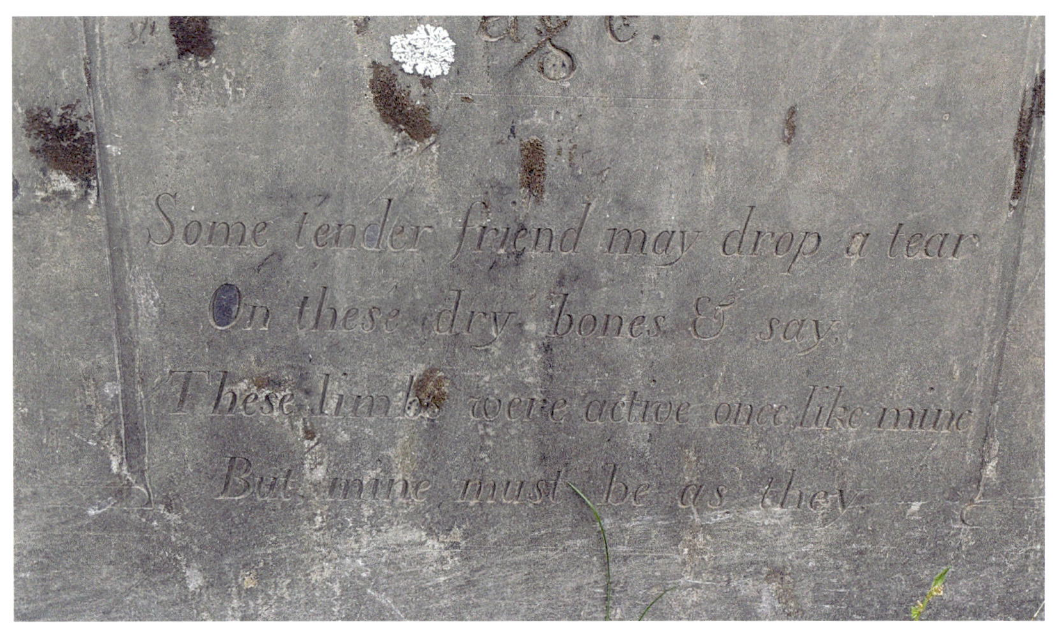

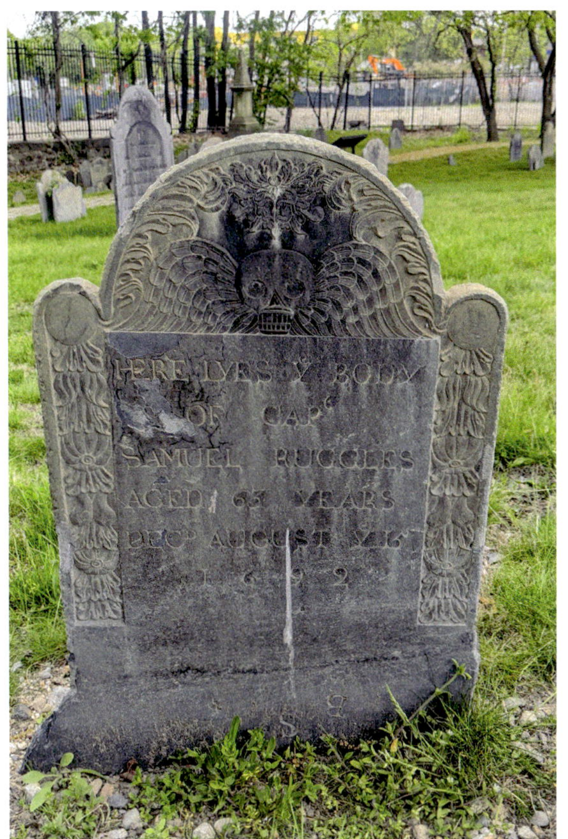

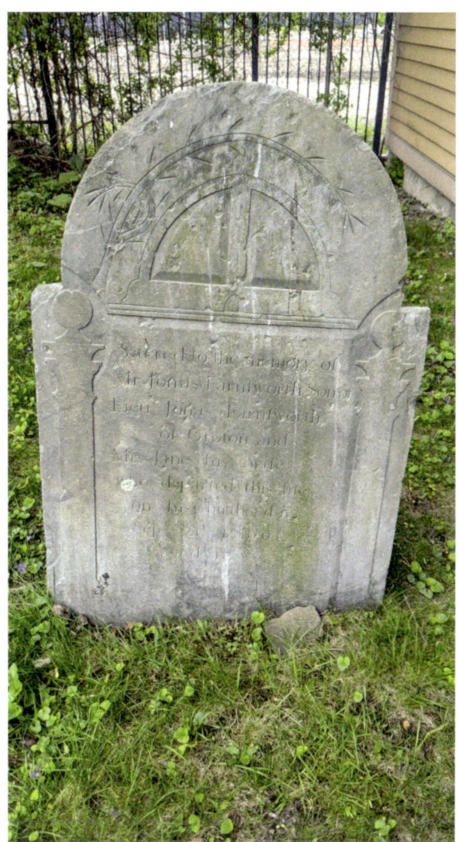

Above left: Eliot Burying Ground is surrounded by a high fence and is largely unseen by the many people commuting nearby.

Above right: More recent stones provide more written information, like this one that informs us that the deceased died on their birthday.

Right: In some instances, different styles of type were used to create a more individual and unique style.

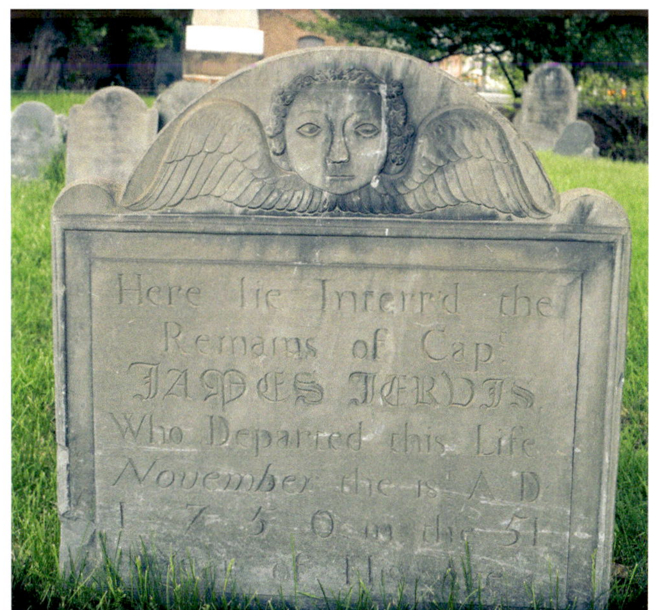

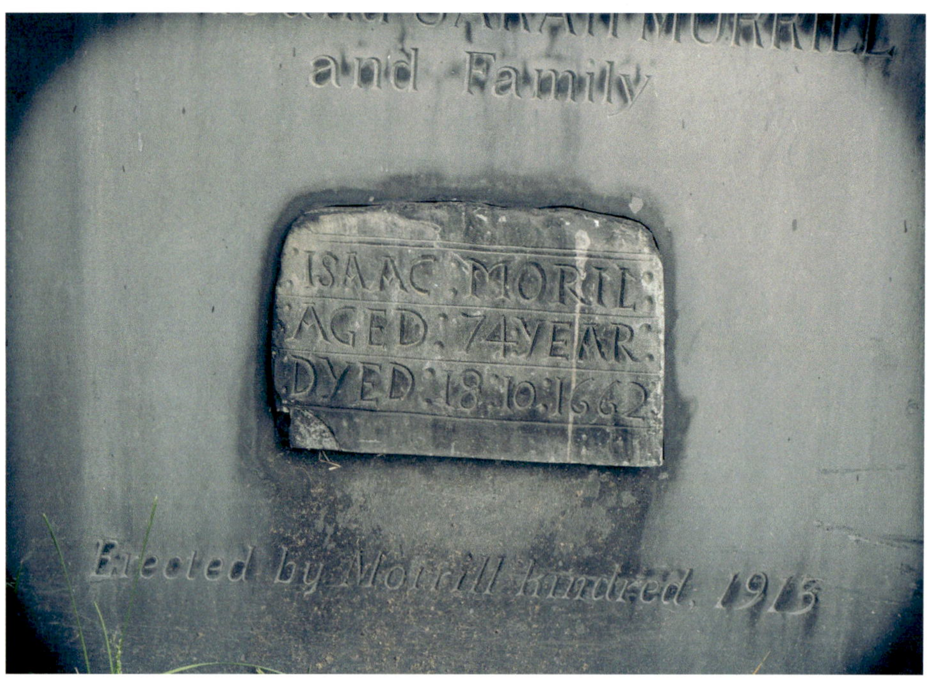

Not all the gravestones remain in one piece. For some, only fragments remain, and in those instances, they can be restored and added to a newer monument.

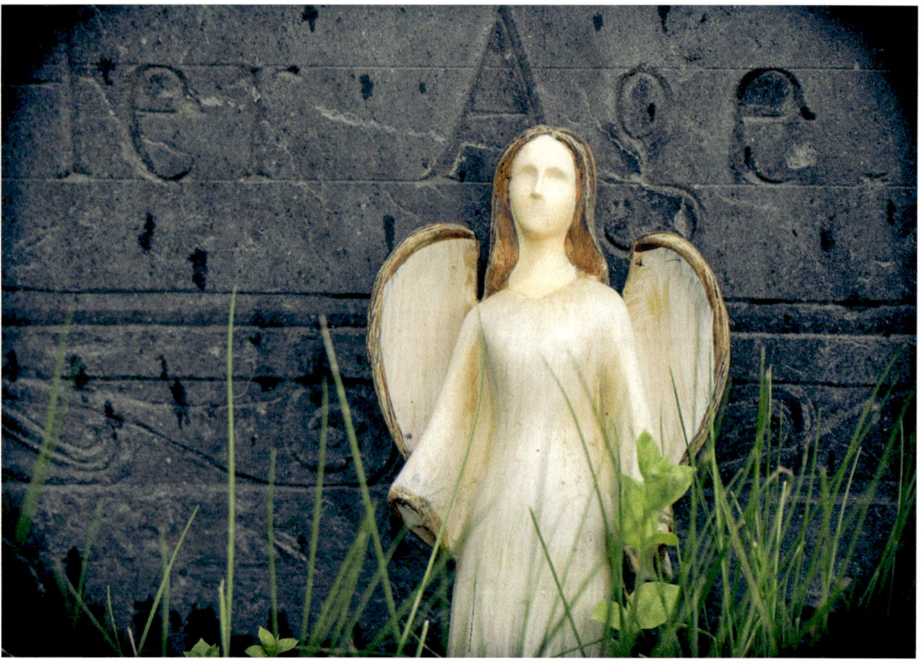

Despite its age, people still leave remembrances for the deceased here at Eliot Burying Ground.

3

PHIPPS STREET BURYING GROUND

Phipps Street Burying Ground is located in the Charlestown neighborhood of Boston. Established in 1630, it is one of the oldest burial grounds in the United States and was used until around 1810. The most famous denizen is John Harvard, the founder of Harvard University. Harvard's original monument has been lost to history, and his exact gravesite remains unknown. In 1828, a 15-foot obelisk was placed in his name, which still prominently stands among the hundreds of tombstones.[1] While many of Boston's earliest burying grounds attempted to modernize their layouts to make them more hospitable to visitors, Phipps Street Burying Ground kept its original layout. The original layout makes searching for specific stones a challenge, but you will be greeted by many fast-jumping rabbits as you explore the grounds.

It is also home to several impressive carvings by the Charleston Stone Cutter, whose work was also seen in King's Chapel Burying Ground. Although the identity of the Charleston Stone Cutter remains unknown, we do know that their work was highly sought after for the intricate and peculiar designs and carvings the artisan created. Many of their works can be found in the Phipps Street Burying Ground, but their most famous carving—that of the printer John Foster—can now be seen within the collection of the Museum Fine Arts in Boston.[2] The Charleston Stone Cutter's legacy lives on through their beautiful and unique creations, which continue to be admired and appreciated by visitors to the grounds.

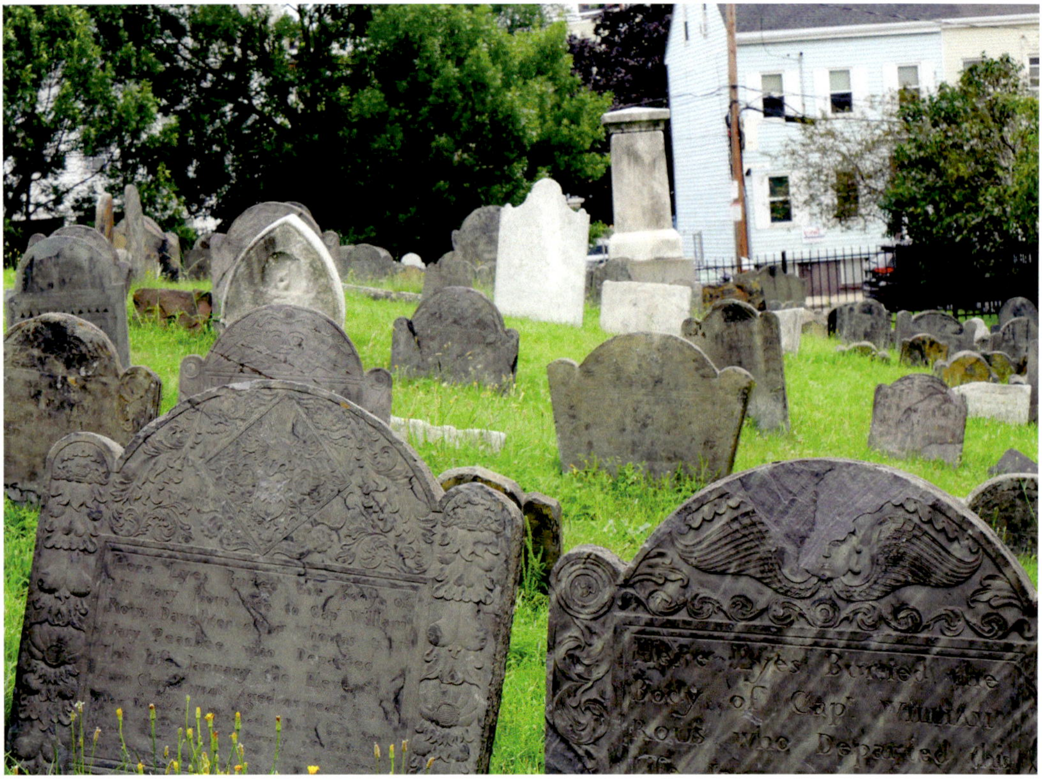

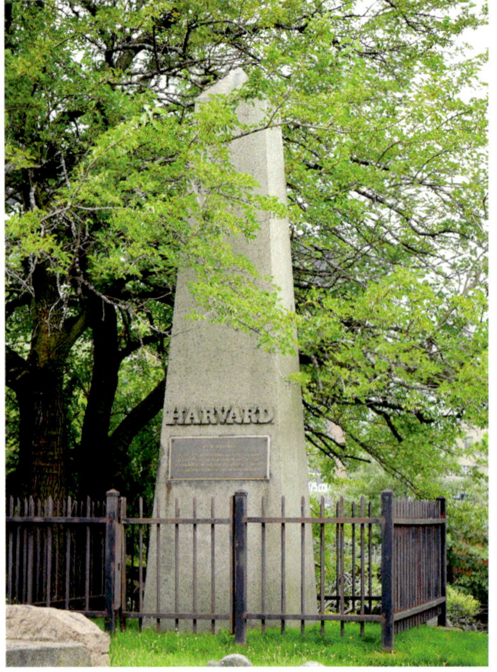

Above: Phipps Street Burying Ground is located in Charleston.

Left: John Harvard was a major benefactor of Cambridge University, which would go on to be named Harvard University later on. Harvard's original burial place is unknown, so this obelisk was added many years after his death.

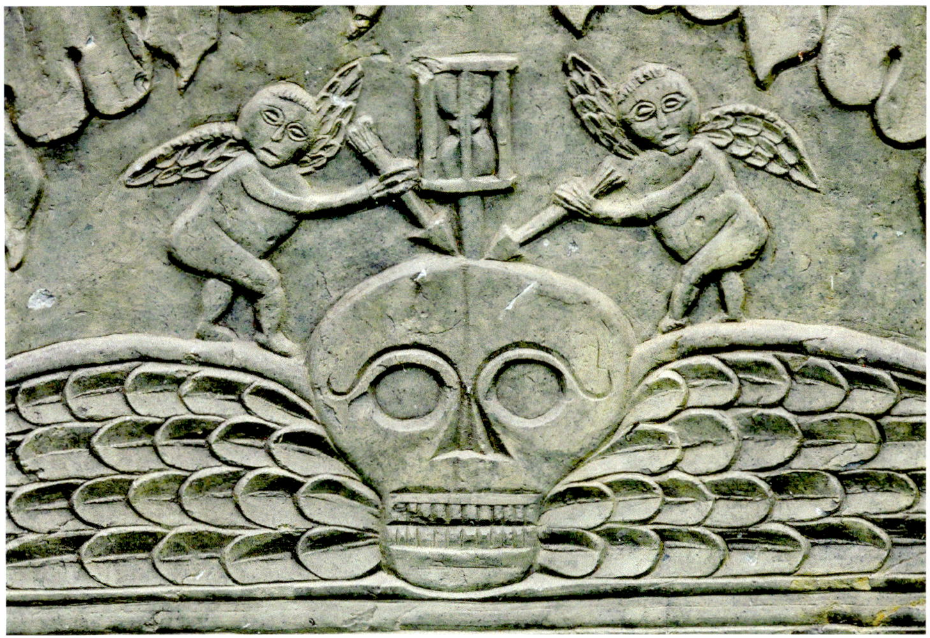

Phipps Street Burying Ground is home to many peculiar symbols, like this one featuring two fat cherubs stabbing a death's head skull with arrows.

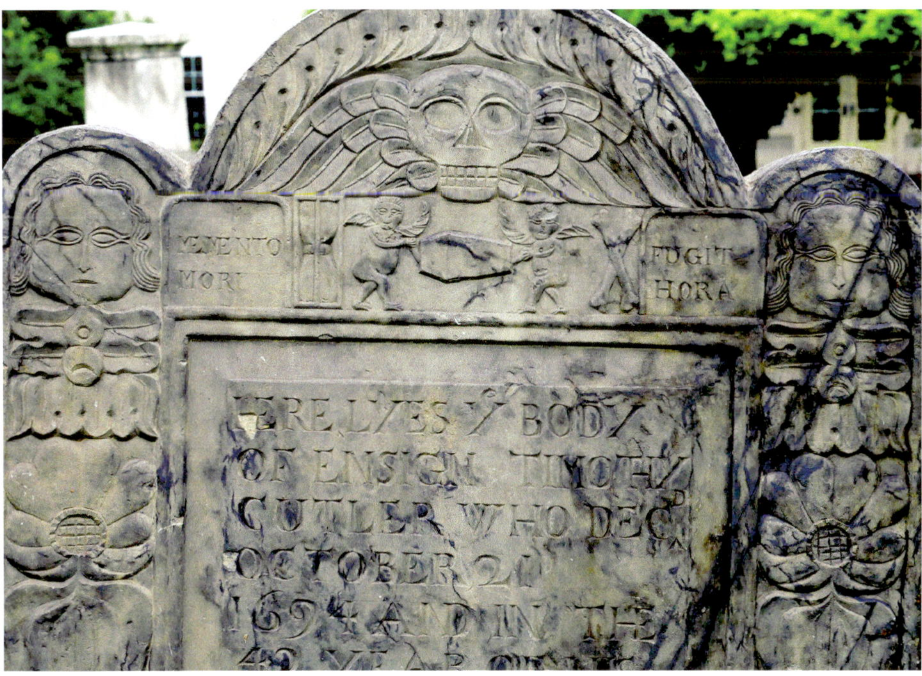

In many instances the stones are practically cluttered with symbols. Most curious in this case are the two chubby angels carrying a casket by hand.

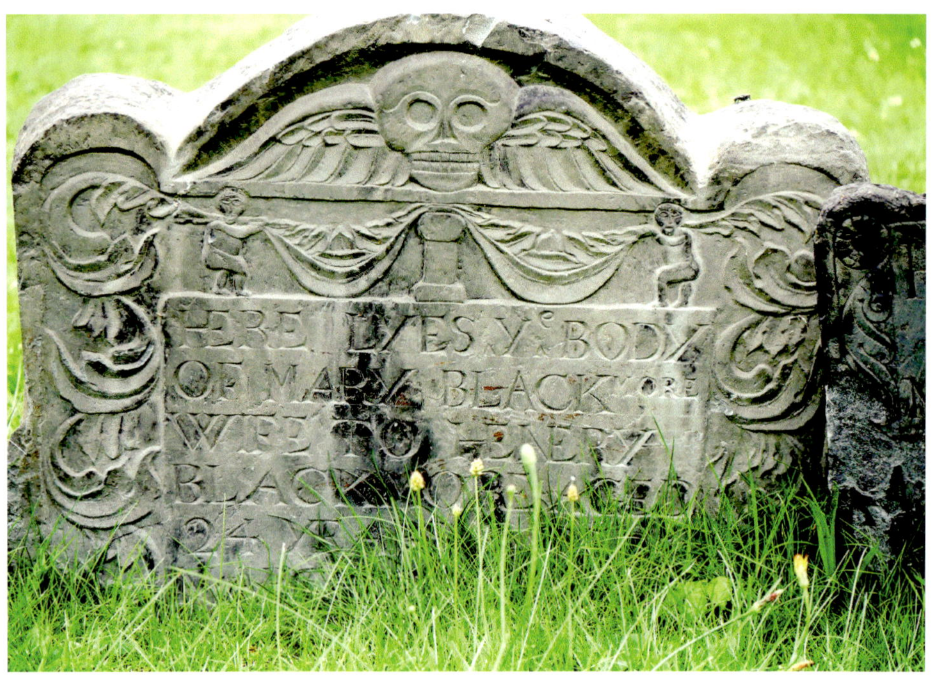

Two bizarre child-like figures unfurl a banner on the grave dedicated to Mary Black.

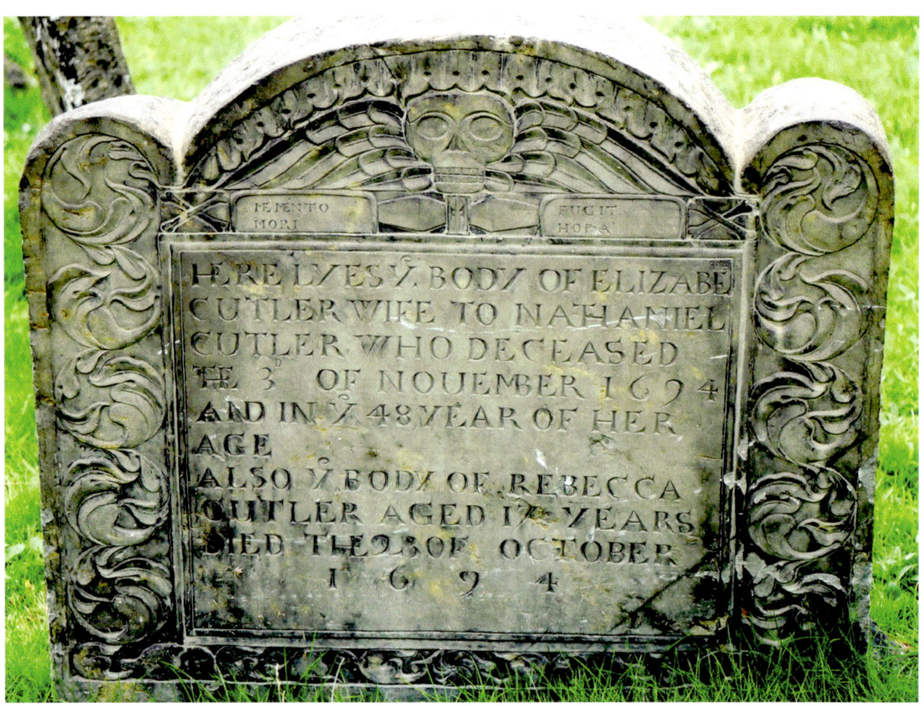

This grave belonging to a mother and daughter features two coffins next to the hourglass of time.

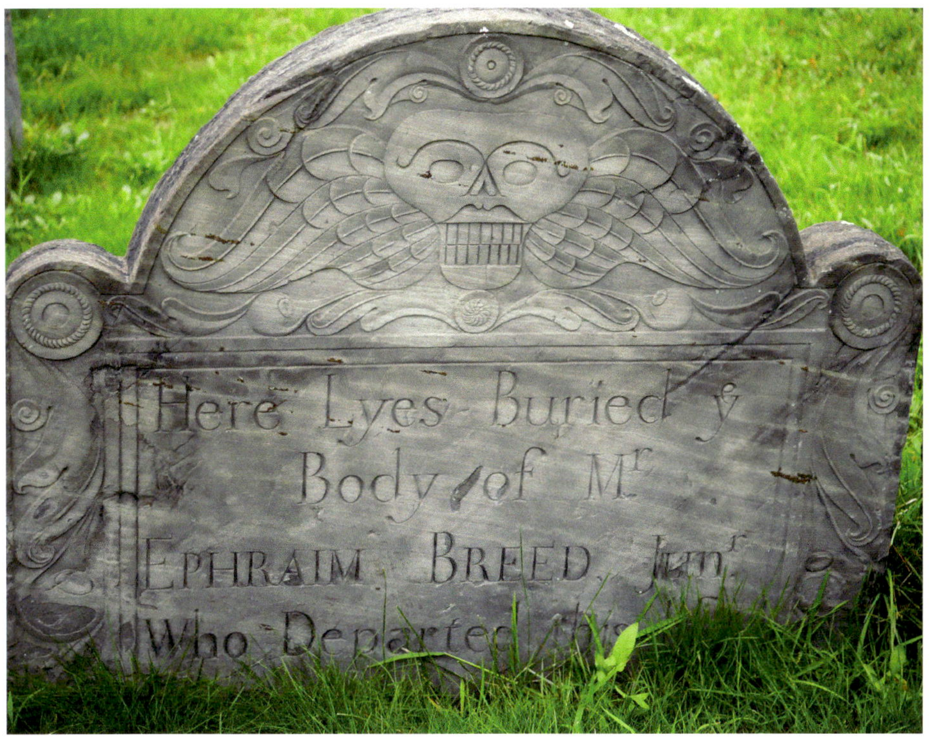

This particularly malevolently grinning skull belongs to the monument dedicated to Ephraim Breed.

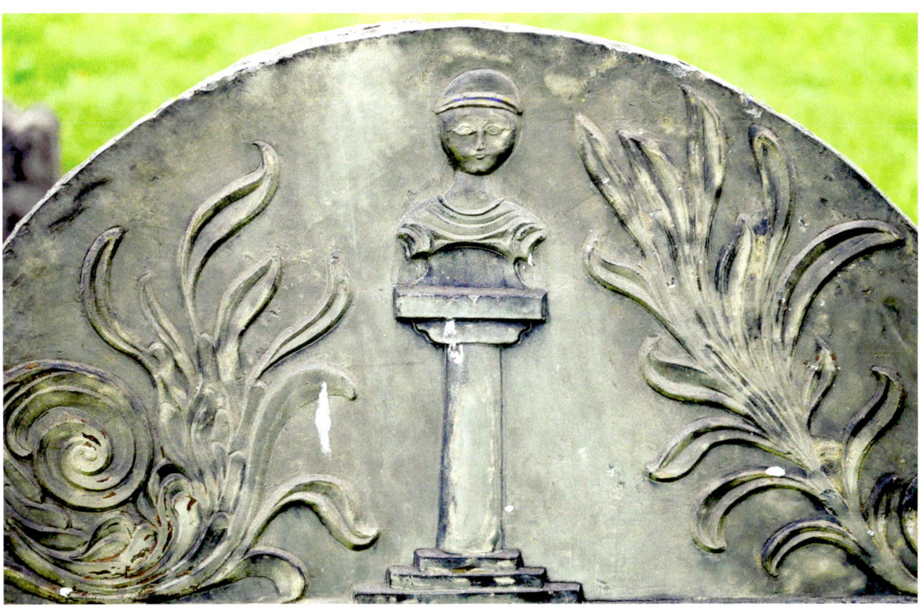

Another peculiar carving is this one featuring a bust of the deceased.

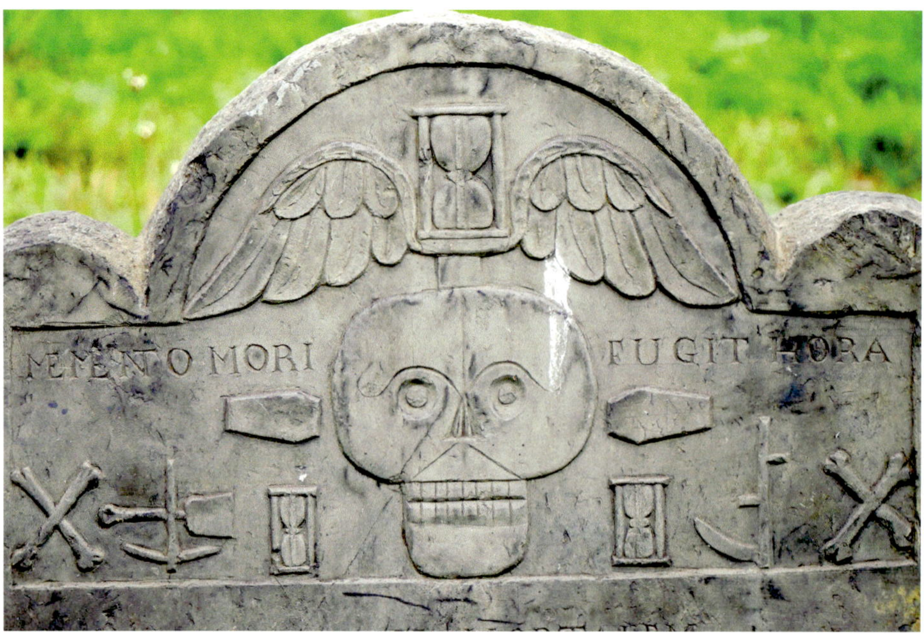

This stone contains many familiar cemetery symbols, including crossbones, an hourglass, a pick and a shovel, scythe, skull, and a winged hourglass. It is one of many stones attributed to the Old Stone Cutter.

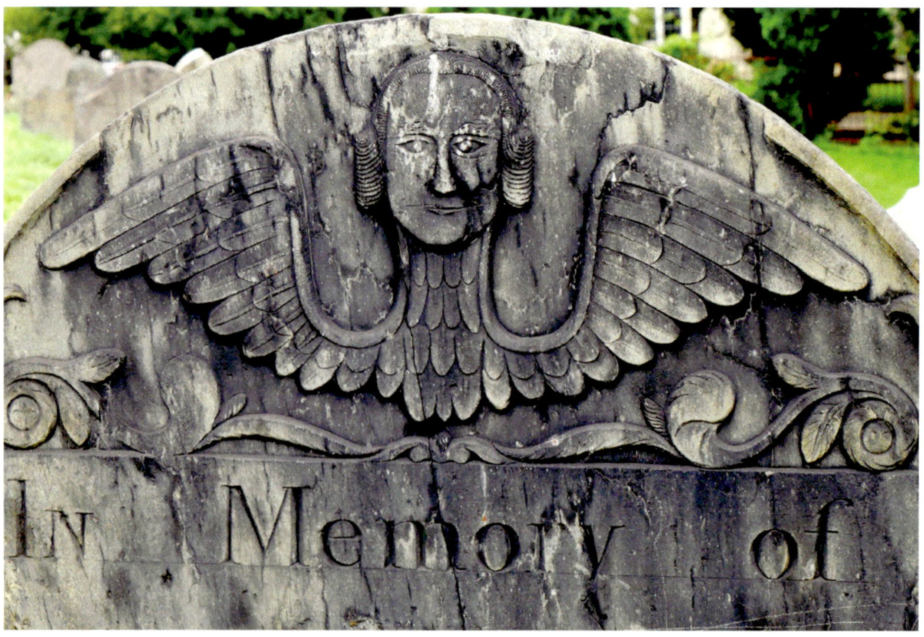

This particular long neck cherub appears more harpy-like than angelic. It adorns the stone dedicated to Captain Stephen Hall, who died at the age of eighty years old.

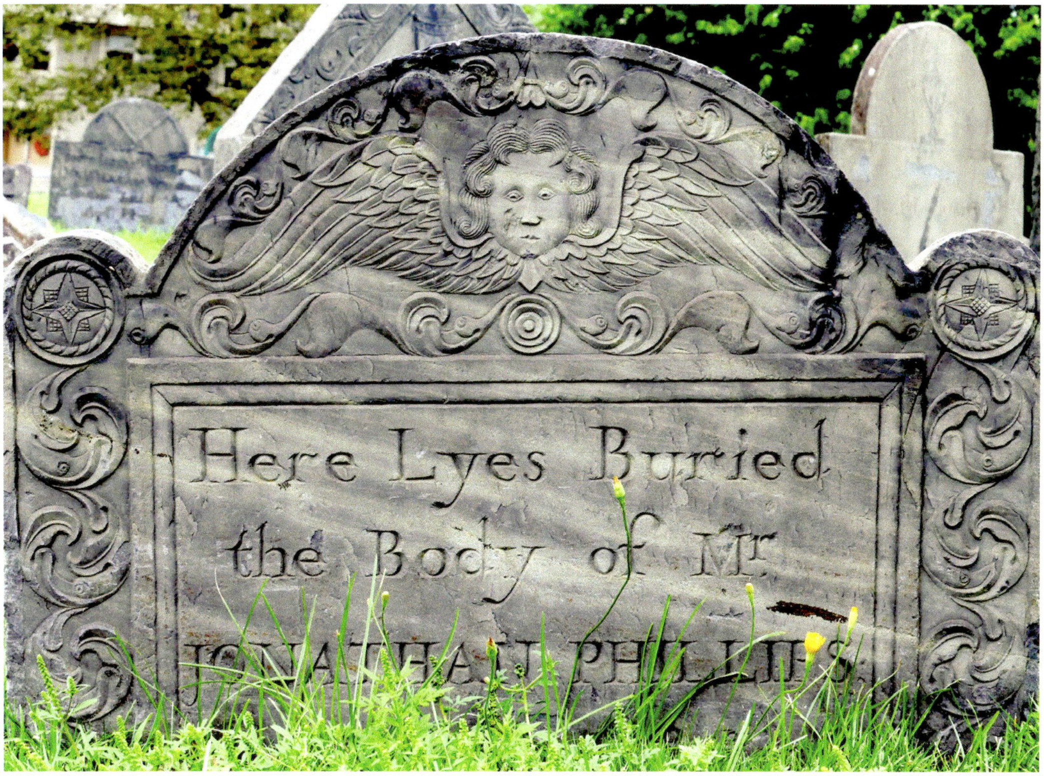

Above: The incredibly elaborate monument dedicated to Jonathan Phillips.

Right: A single stone is dedicated to the four young children of Samuel and Sarah Oliver. The children all died before they were five years old. The inscription reads: "Just like an early rose, Were seen an infants bud. But sudden oft before it blows, Death lays it in the tomb."

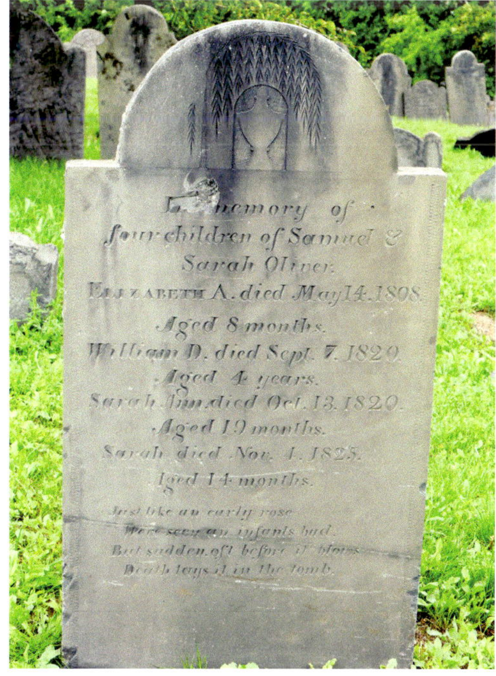

4

Copp's Hill Burying Ground

Located at 45 Hull Street and Snowhill Road in Boston's North End is Copp's Hill Burying Ground. Established in 1659, the burying ground is home to over 10,000 souls.[1] Its picturesque hillside location overlooking the harbor made it a strategic location during the American Revolution. Now, the historical tombstones of Copp's Hill are surrounded by traffic signs and modern apartment buildings, including Boston's "Skinny House" located directly across the street.

Copp's Hill Burying Ground is made up of numerous scattered tombstones but is also home to the prominent Mather family tomb. Made of a tall brick table-like structure, the tomb is the final burial place for Cotton and Increase Mather, who died within a few years of one another. Increase Mather was a well-known Puritan minister, who published *Remarkable Providences,* which was an essay of facts pertaining to spirit rappings, apparitions, the Devil, and of course, witchcraft. Increase's book had a tremendous effect on his son, Cotton, who was a major participant and defender of the Salem Witch Trials.

A number of important figures in American history are buried within Copp's Hill. Robert Newman, the man responsible for hanging lanterns for Paul Revere's famous ride, is buried here. Two monuments, one being a tribute monument that was added later, are dedicated to Prince Hall. Prince Hall was an abolitionist and founder of the Prince Hall Freemasonry. Hall was one of the most important Black leaders in Boston and a huge supporter of equal rights in education and the Back-to-Africa Movement.

Surrounded by the footprints of many enthusiastic field trips is the grave dedicated to Captain Daniel Malcolm. Malcolm died in 1769 at the age of forty-four and was a strong supporter of the famed Sons of Liberty. An active and loud opponent of British authorities, he was also a known smuggler responsible for illegally importing over sixty casks of wine without paying any taxes.[2] When confronted by the British authorities, he gathered over 100 men to surround them to help successfully intimidate them and drop the search.

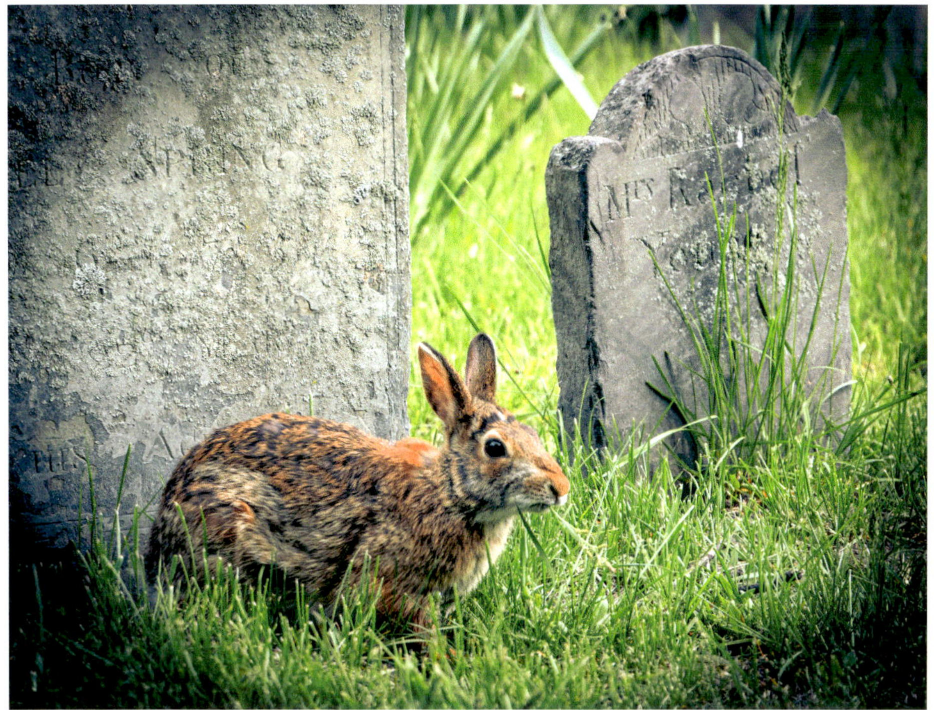

Despite the tourists, many rabbits call the burying ground home.

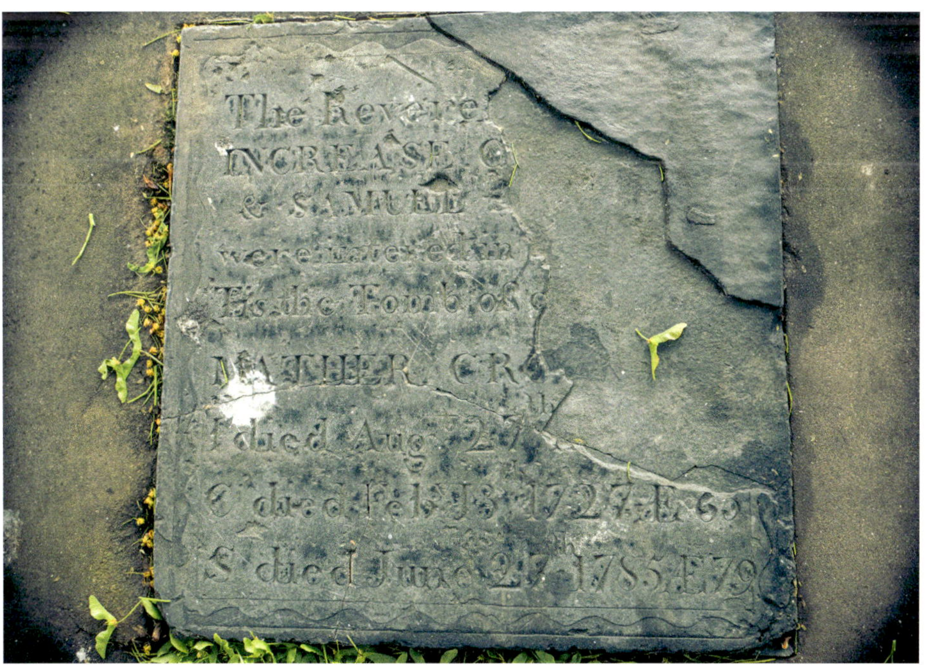

The marker for Increase Mather has been substantially damaged over the years.

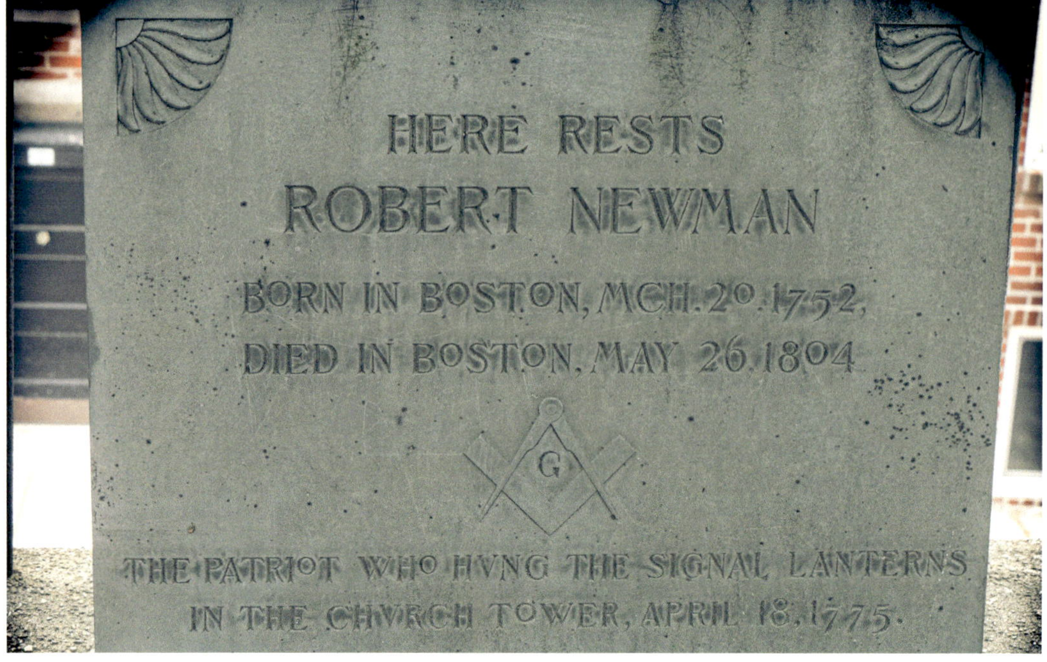

Above: In addition to being the burial place for Paul Revere, Boston is also home to Robert Newman, the man who helped light the way for that faithful ride.

Below left: The newer memorial to Prince Hall dwarfs his previous one seen directly behind.

Below right: The original memorial dedicated to Prince Hall has sustained some damage.

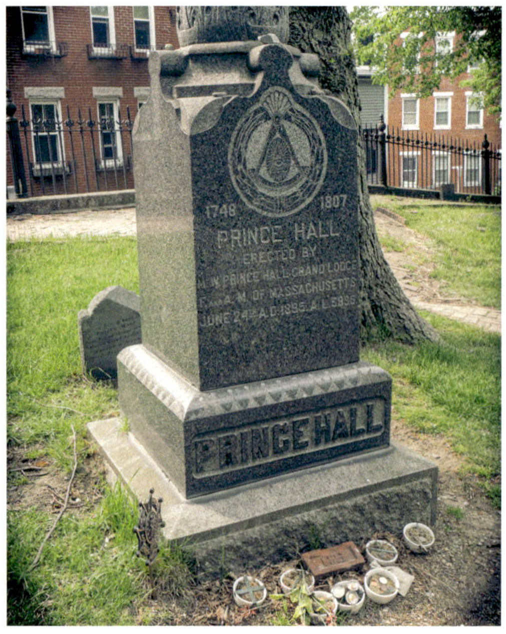

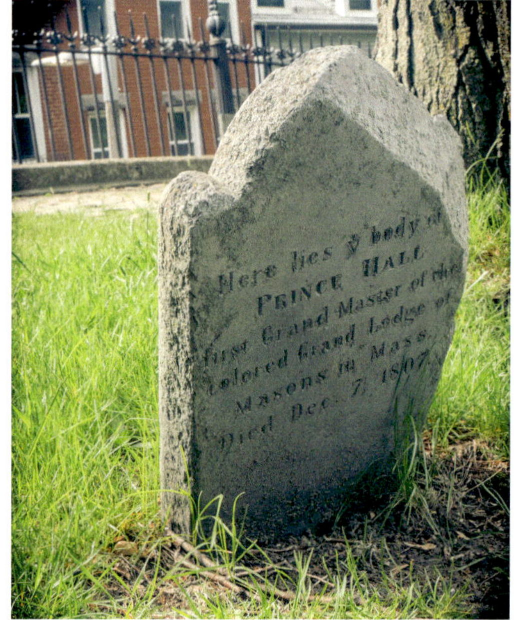

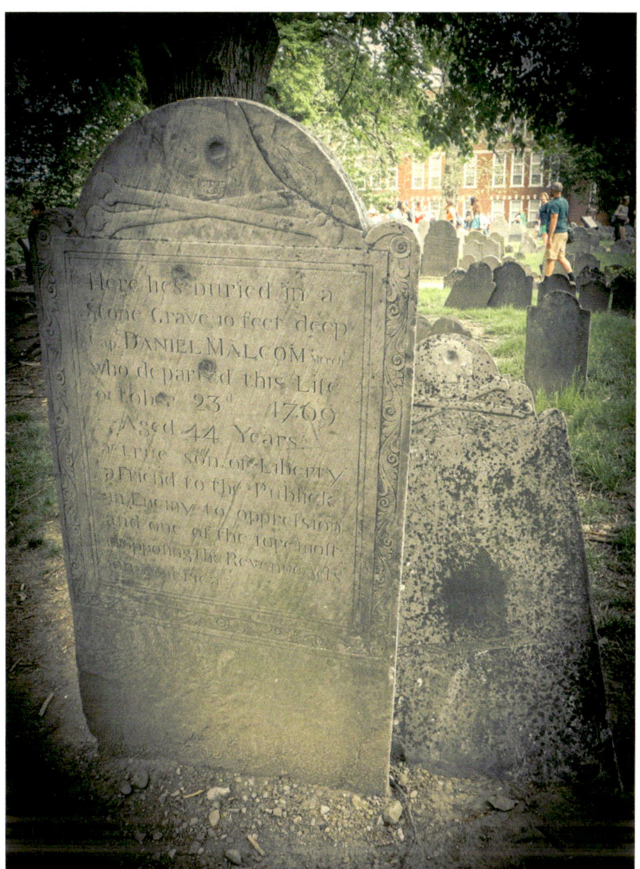

The tombstone dedicated to Daniel Malcolm, patriot and wine smuggler, is rumored to have been used by British soldiers for target practice to express their disdain.

Malcolm had requested a few provisions for when he died. Anticipating that his remains would be a target due to his past hostilities with the British authorities, he requested that his body be buried ten feet deep. While his remains were not necessarily disturbed (that we know of) one can see clear imprints of musket balls on his tombstone. It is said that in an act of defiance, British soldiers used Malcolm's stone for target practice. His stone reads:

> Here lies buried in a stone grave 10 feet deep, Capt. Daniel Malcolm, Merchant who departed this life October 23rd, 1769 age 44 years. A true son of Liberty. An enemy to oppression and one of the foremost in opposing the Revenue Acts on America.

There are also thousands of Black Bostonians buried in unmarked graves along Snowhill Street. These were former residents of Boston's first Black community, and the first free Black community in the United States, commonly known as New Guinea.[3] There are an additional 272 tombs—many with faded inscriptions. Phyllis Wheatley, the first published African American author, is reportedly buried within the grounds, although she lacks a proper tombstone.

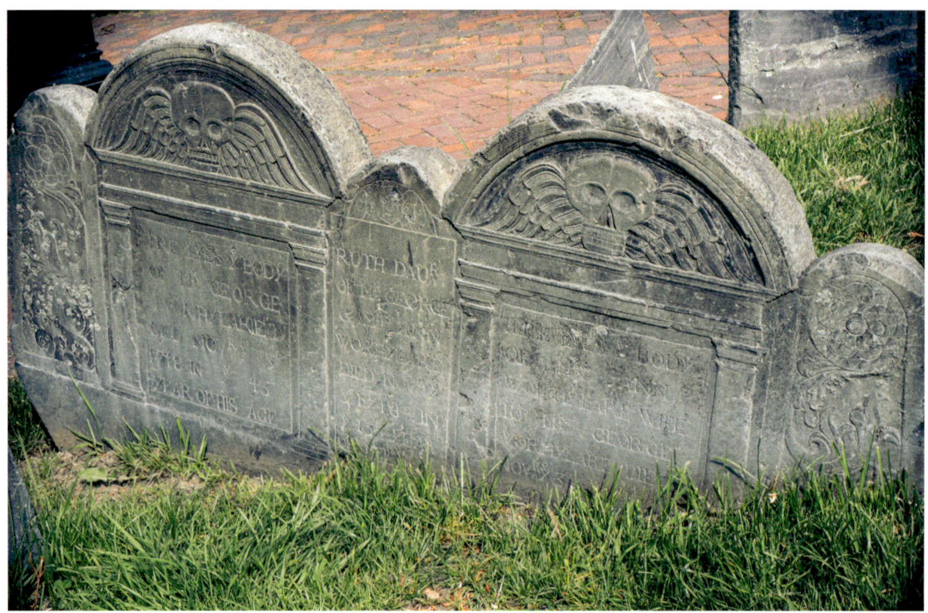

George Worthylake was the keeper of the Boston Light, Boston's famous lighthouse. In 1718, he, his wife, and their daughter, Ruth, drowned on their return to Little Brewster Island after attending church.

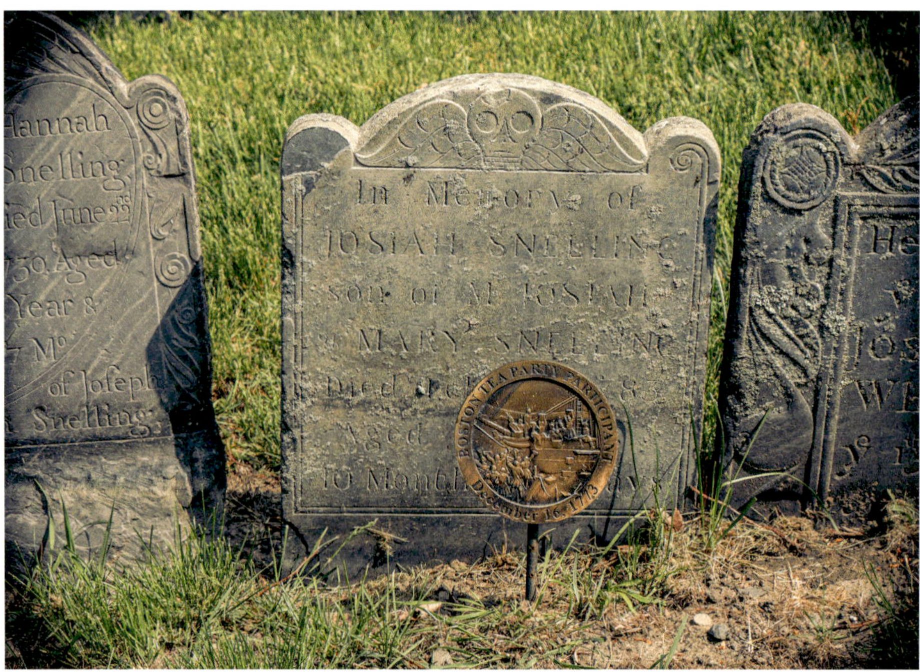

Many of the tombstones have these small circular plaques acknowledging their participation during the famous Boston Tea Party.

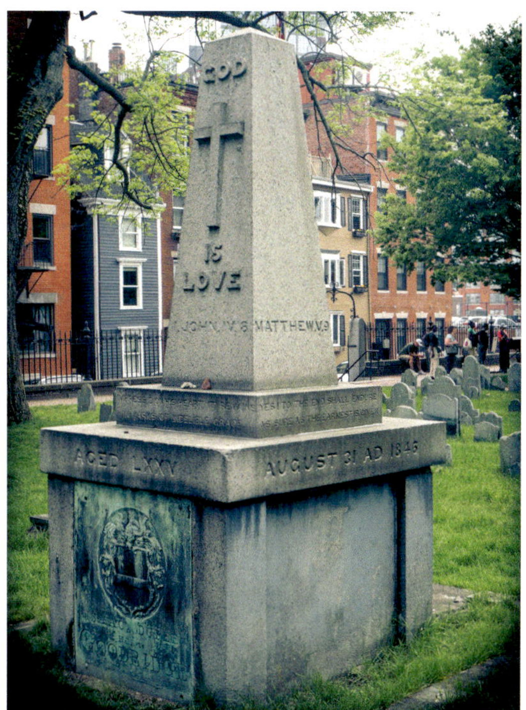

Right: One of the rare obelisk-style monuments within Copp's Hill Burying Ground.

Below: This stunning headstone depicts two angels holding onto an urn topped with a death's head.

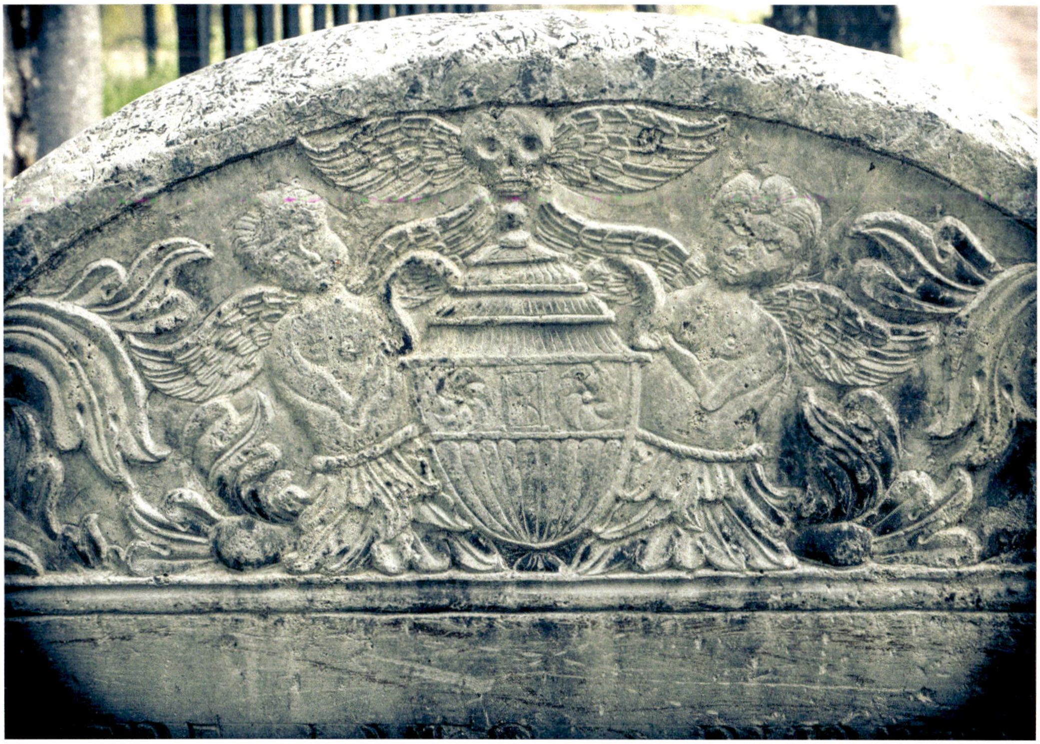

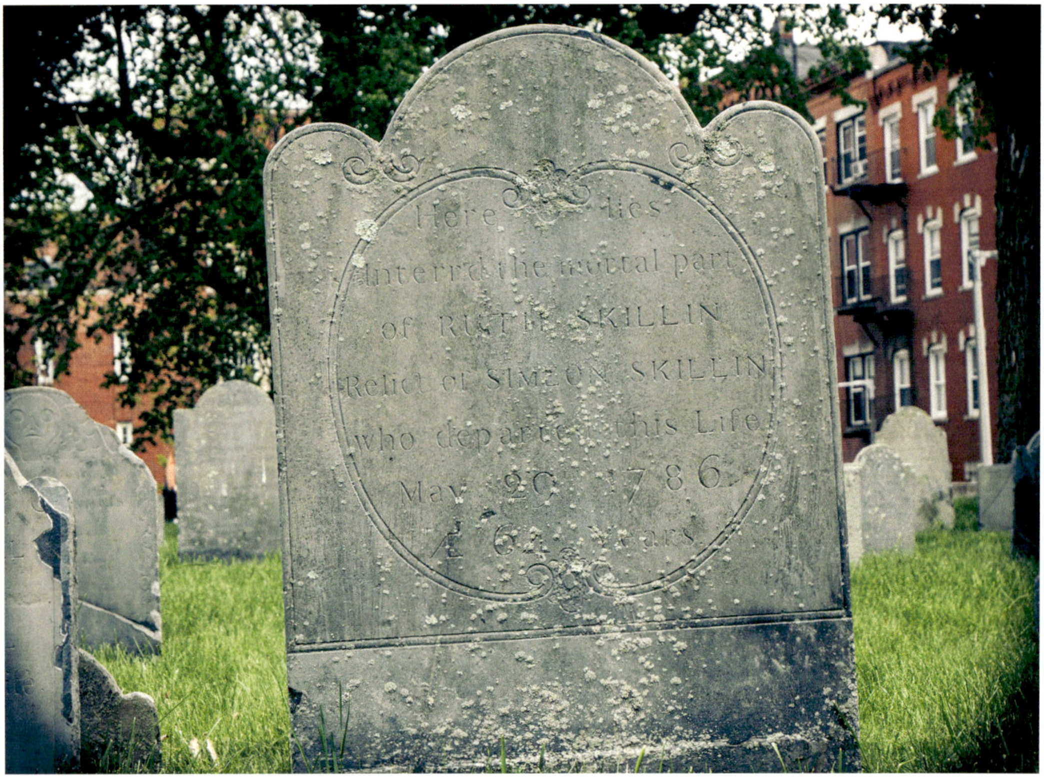

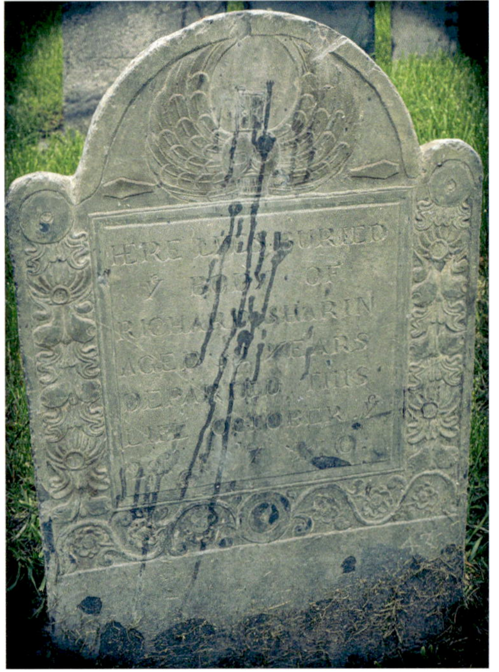

Above: Many of the inscriptions are particularly macabre, like this one that describes the deceased as the "mortal part of Ruth Skillin."

Left: Death's head with wings outspread and symmetrical coffin design.

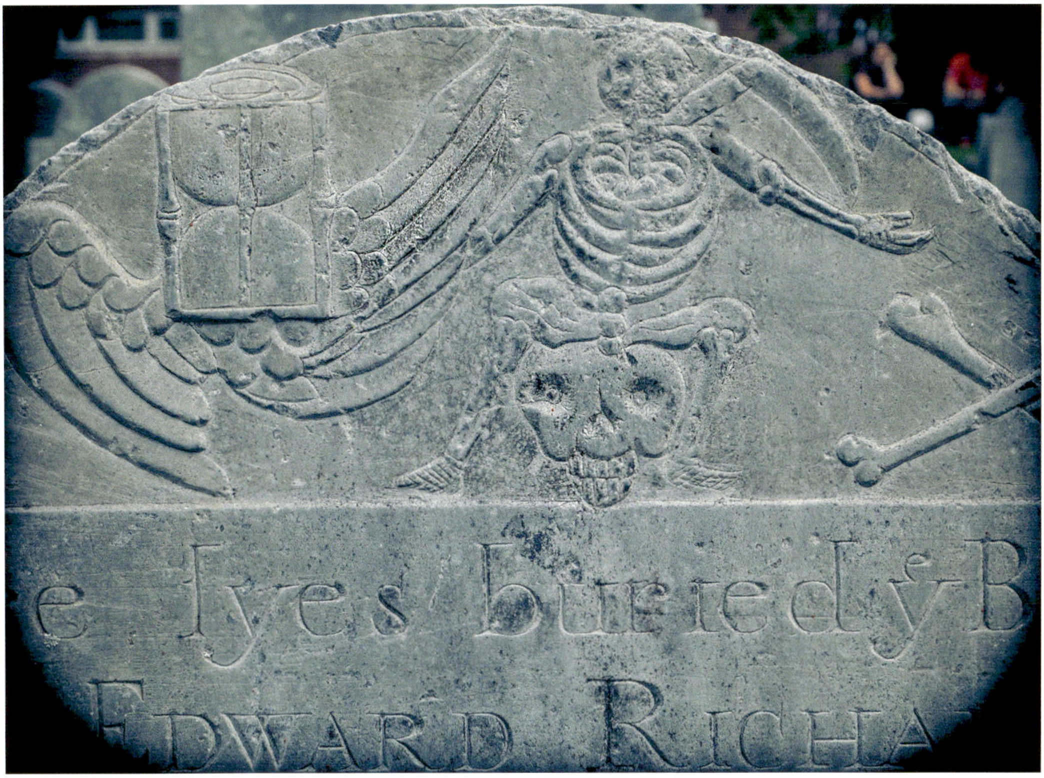

Above: Death seated on a skull while the hourglass of time flies away.

Right: In some cases, some of the markers have nothing more than a name.

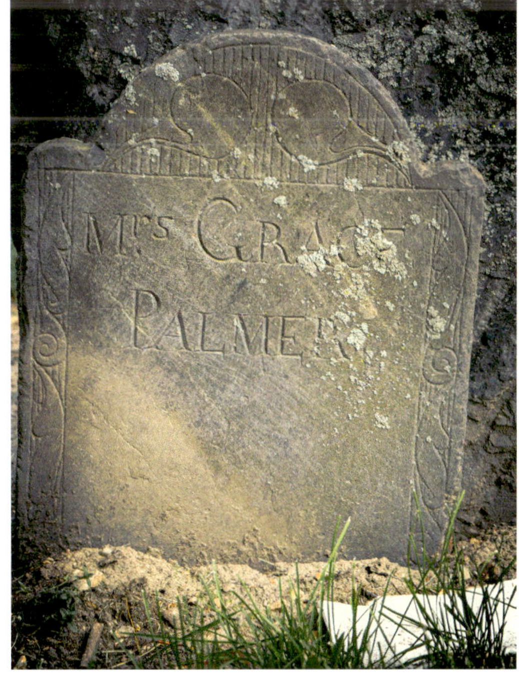

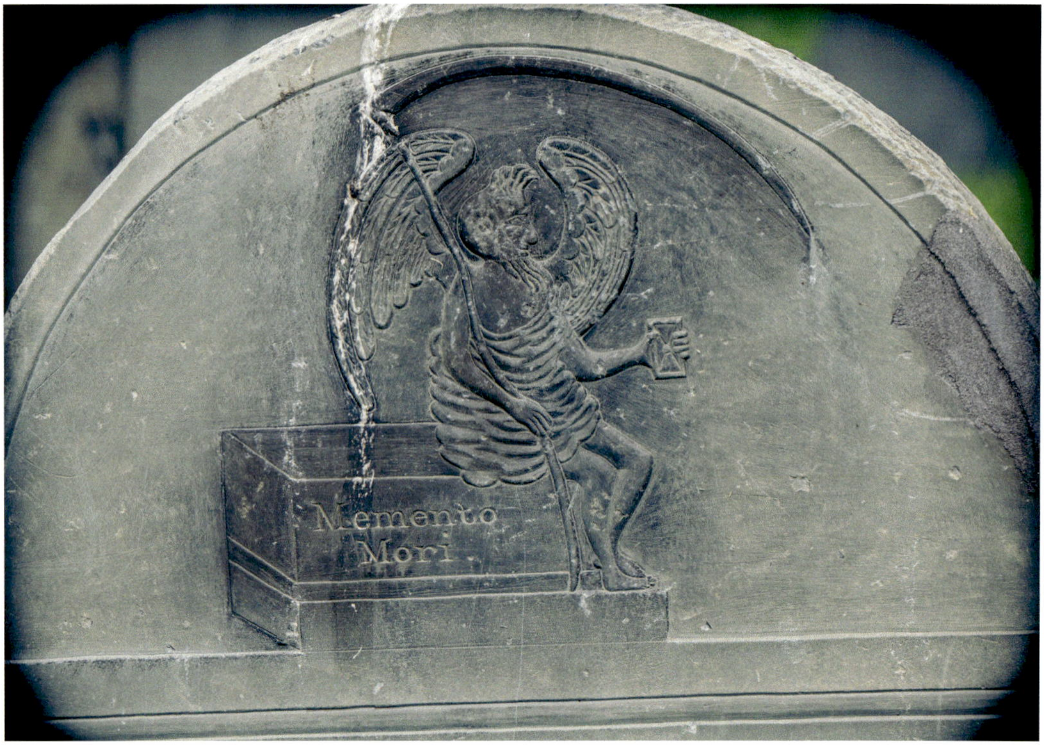

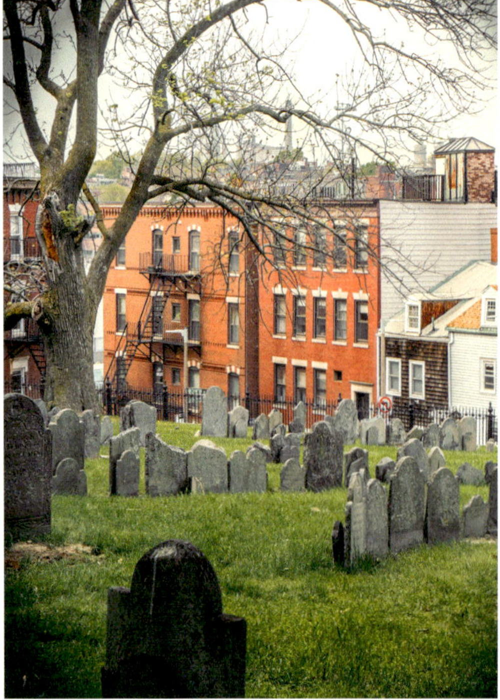

Above: A particularly cheeky depiction of Father Time, scythe in hand, sitting down as he waits for the hour glass of time to run out.

Left: Copp's Hill Burying Ground is on an actual hill overlooking the water.

5

Granary Burying Ground

Trampled by hundreds of eager tourists a day, Granary Burying Ground is a veritable "who's who" of the American Revolution. Located on Tremont Street, Granary Burying Ground was established in 1660 as a means to ease the severe overcrowding at nearby King's Chapel Burying Ground. Granary has over 2,000 stone markers and is home to over 5,000 permanent residents.[1] Originally a Puritan burial ground, the stones are filled with ominous death's heads, skulls, and flying effigies.

Granary Burying Ground has had a number of revisions and restorations since it was first established. In 1720, the grounds were expanded, and fifteen additional tombs were added. Granary was originally similar in layout to other burial grounds on the Freedom Trail, with the stones haphazardly placed. Originally part of the Boston Common, landscaping was done by local livestock. As technology changed and the livestock population diminished, Granary was reorganized into the cleanly organized lines of stones seen today in an effort to accommodate space for modern lawnmowers.[2] Later additions including trees, fencing, and the elaborate Egyptian revival archway were added in an attempt to make the grounds more welcoming and hospitable for visitors.

In 2011, Granary underwent a substantial $300,000 restoration project.[3] The paths were repaved to offer more space for the influx of students and tourists that visit each day. The repaving has offered wider paths and large observation spaces for the many well-known historical figures. In an effort to keep visitors on the designated paths and less likely to alter and deface the tombstones, additional fences have also been added. These more recent additions, even the most adept photographer will have difficulty trying to photograph the stones without an excited tourist in the way.

Prominently featured at the center is a large granite obelisk designating the Franklin family plot. While many of the Franklin family are here, including Josiah and Aviah Franklin, their famous son, Benjamin, is not (he's buried in Philadelphia). Not far behind the Franklins is a memorial dedicated to none other than Paul Revere, whose famous midnight ride warned of approaching British forces. Revere's grave is a favorite for visitors, usually covered with coins and various offerings, and surrounded by people taking photographs. Granary Burying Ground is also home to other American Revolutionaries, including John Hancock, Robert Treat Paine, and Samuel Adams, all

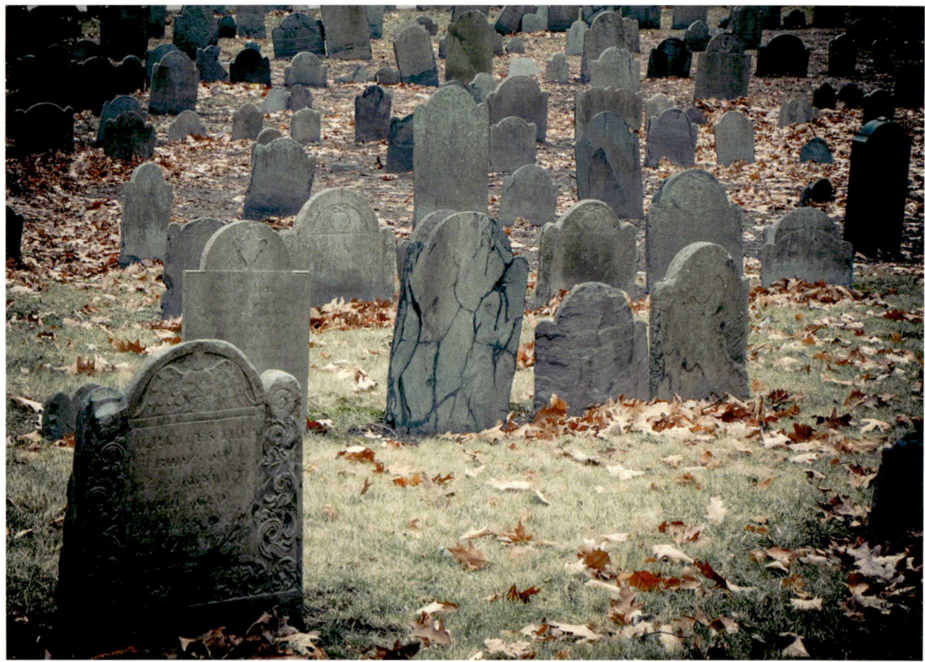

The tightly packed Granary Burying Ground.

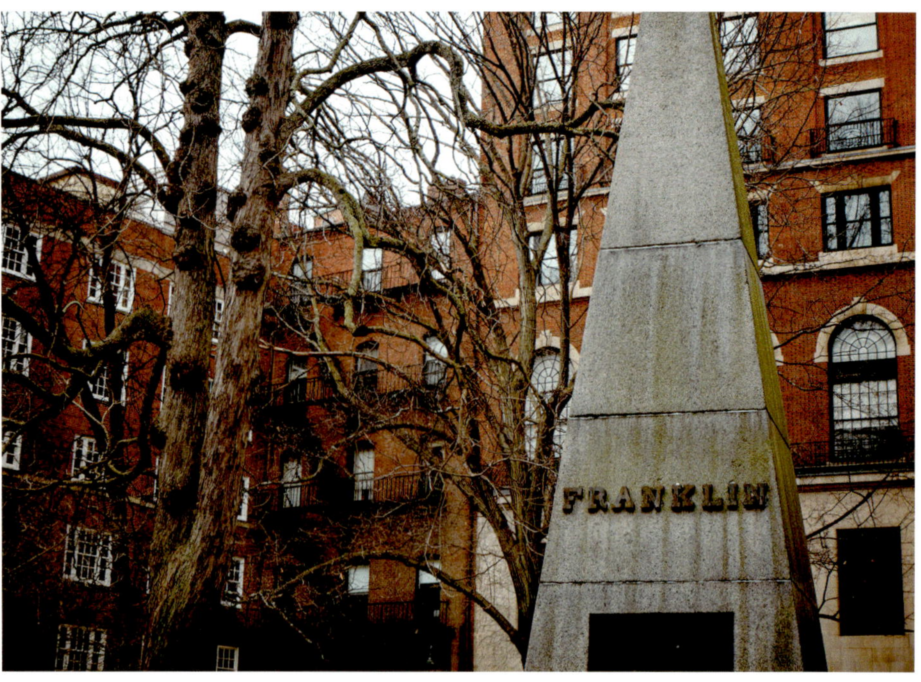

Centrally located is the large monument dedicated to the parents of founding father, Benjamin Franklin.

signers of the Declaration of Independence. Crispus Attucks and multiple victims from the infamous Boston Massacre are also buried within the grounds.

There is no shortage of intricate monuments at Granary Burying Ground. The triangular-shaped memorial dedicated to the four Neal children is notable for its intense detail, especially on the individually carved feathers on the wings on the death's head. None of the Neal children buried here lived for longer than eighteen months. The youngest died at three days old, likely a victim of smallpox, which swept through Boston in the 1600s.[4] The parent's intense sadness is exhibited clearly within the many symbols seen on the conjoined monument. In addition to the elaborate death's head, the stone also features an hourglass, crossbones, and a shovel. The words *TEMPUS EDAX RERUM* ("time, devourer of all things") can be seen on the top of the stone.

The Stillman and Binney tomb is equally as fascinating and even more elaborate. Two grinning grim reapers wearing flowing robes and laurels over their heads are seen on either side. Each one holds a scythe, with their bony heads leaning on their skeletal hands—as if patiently waiting to deliver the next soul. The posture of the skeletal figures is indicative of a passive figure of Death, meaning that it comes to us all sooner or later and they need only wait.

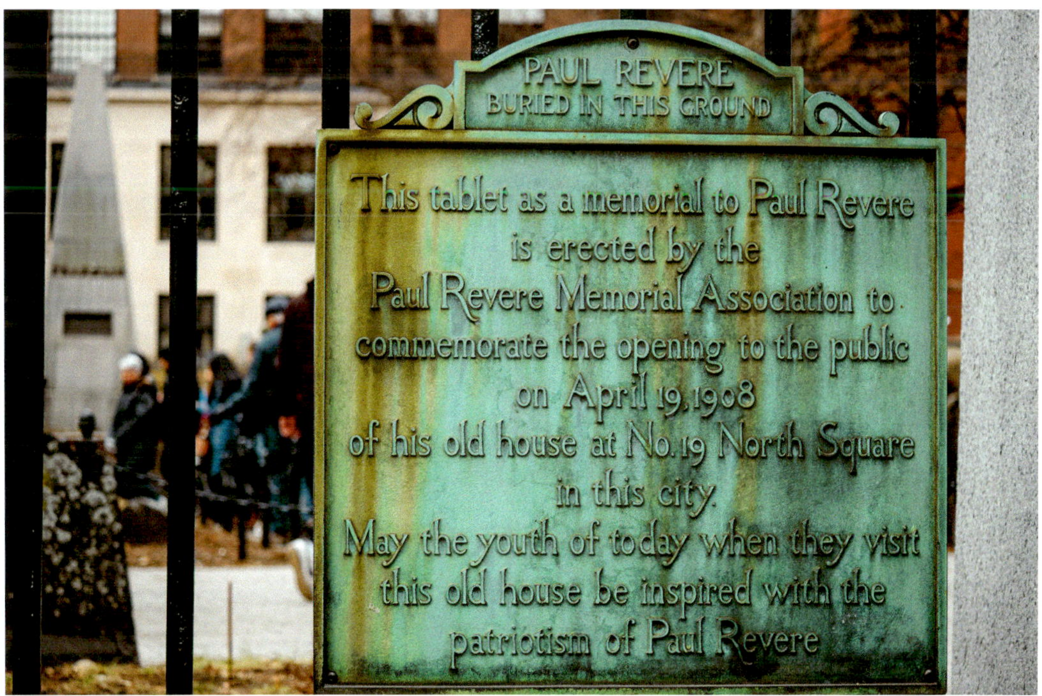

Plaque dedicated to Paul Revere.

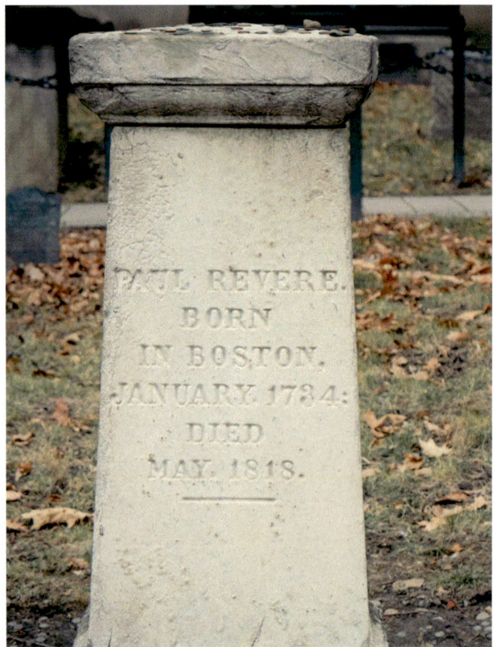

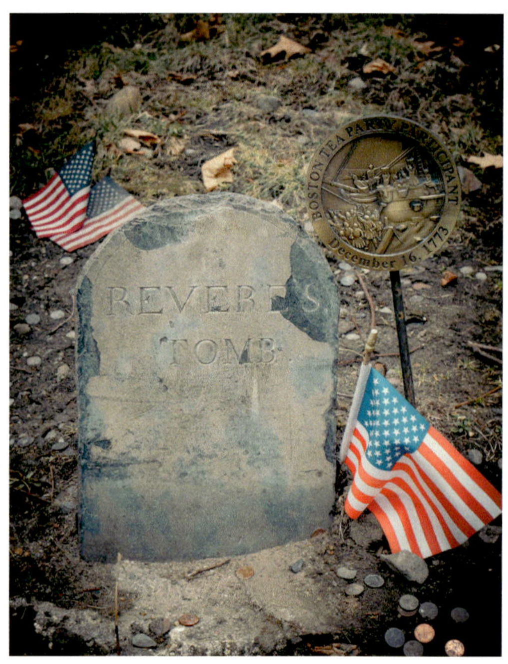

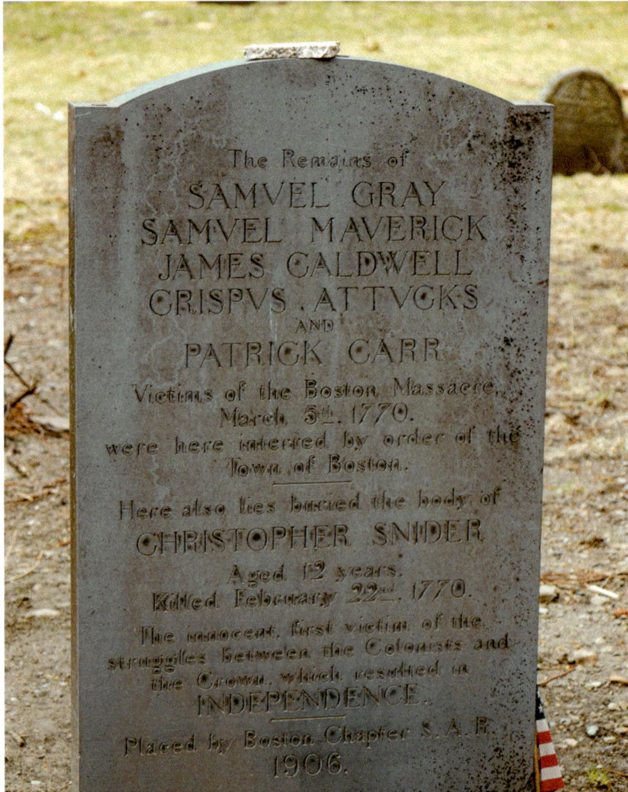

Above left: Many visitors leave coins in remembrance, like those seen on top of Paul Revere's stone.

Above right: Meanwhile, the original marker for Revere's tomb is much smaller in comparison.

Left: Many of the victims of the Boston Massacre are interred within Granary Burying Ground, including Crispus Attucks and Christopher Seider, an eleven-year-old boy who died in the protests leading up to the massacre.

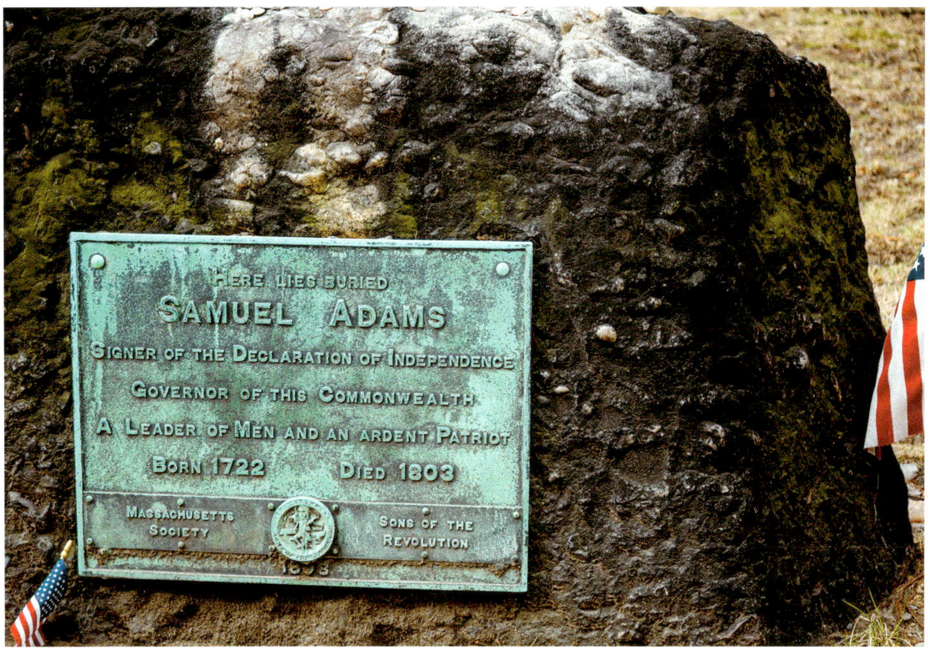

Plaque and monument dedicated to Samuel Adams, signer of the Declaration of Independence and noted beer inspiration.

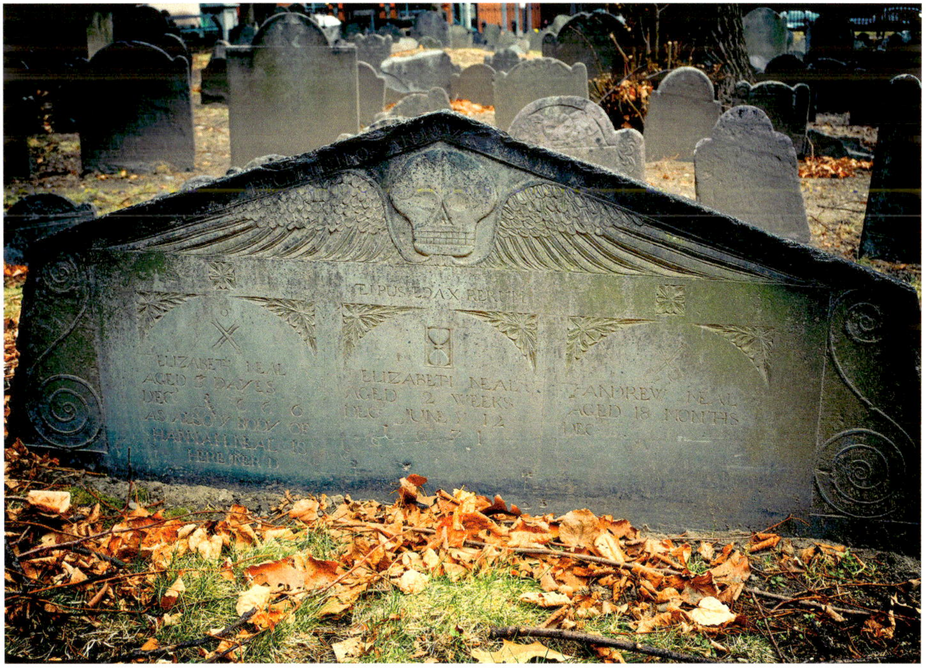

The large triangular shaped monument dedicated to the Neal children, attributed to the Old Stone Cutter.

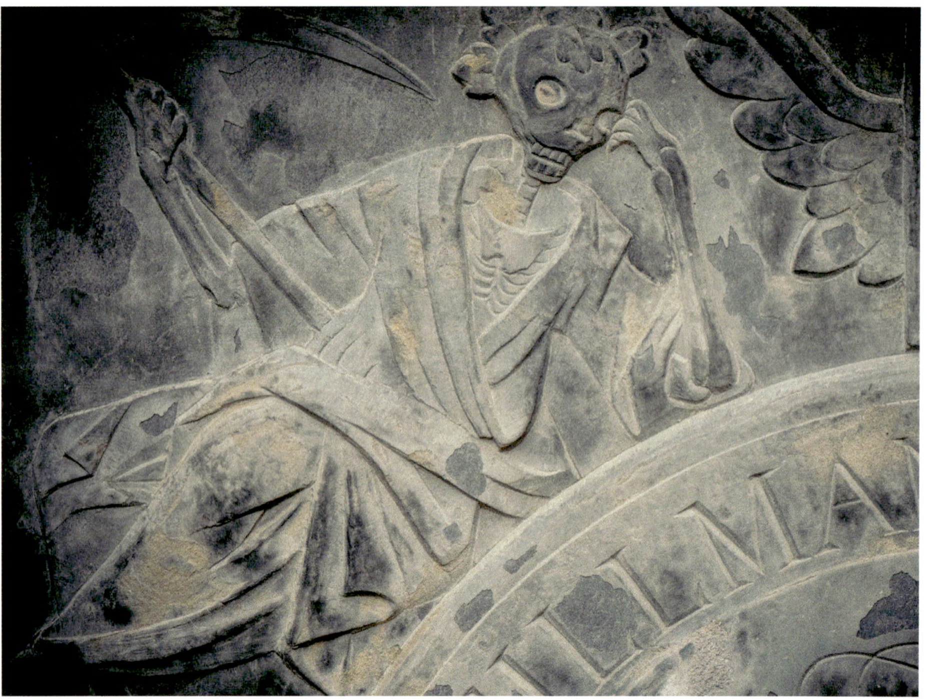

Death patiently waits.

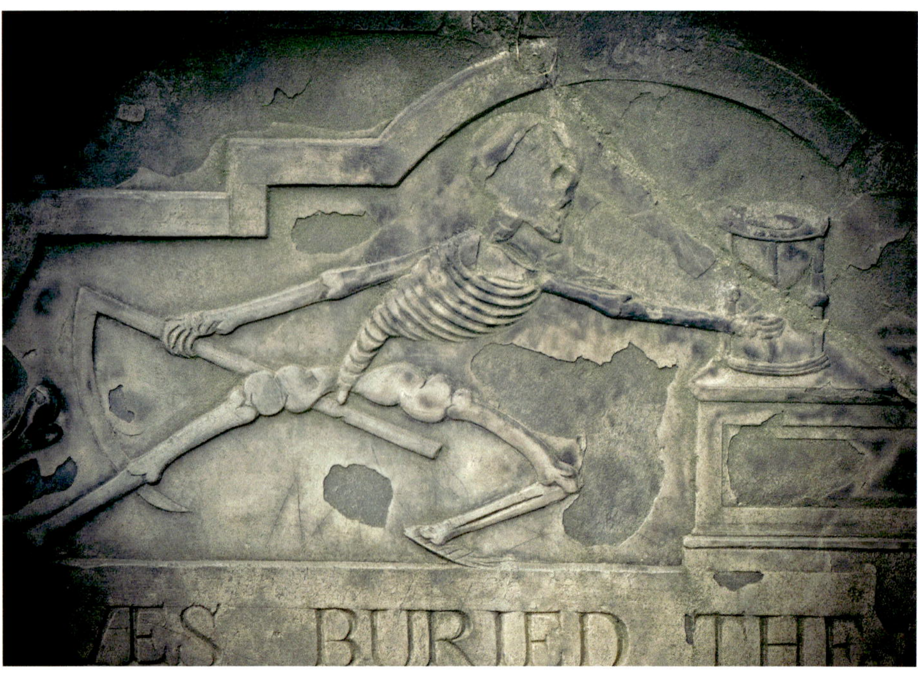

Death stealing the hourglass of time; note the lack of hip bone on the skeletal frame.

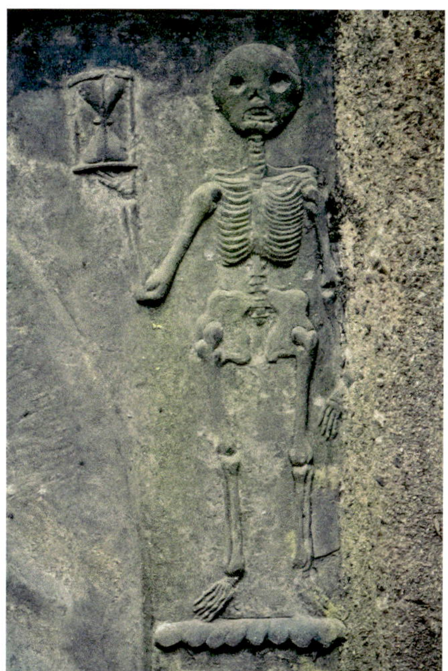

Right: Another deathly skeleton with a visible reminder of our limited time.

Below: The skull and crossbones is a popular symbol among early eighteenth-century tombstones.

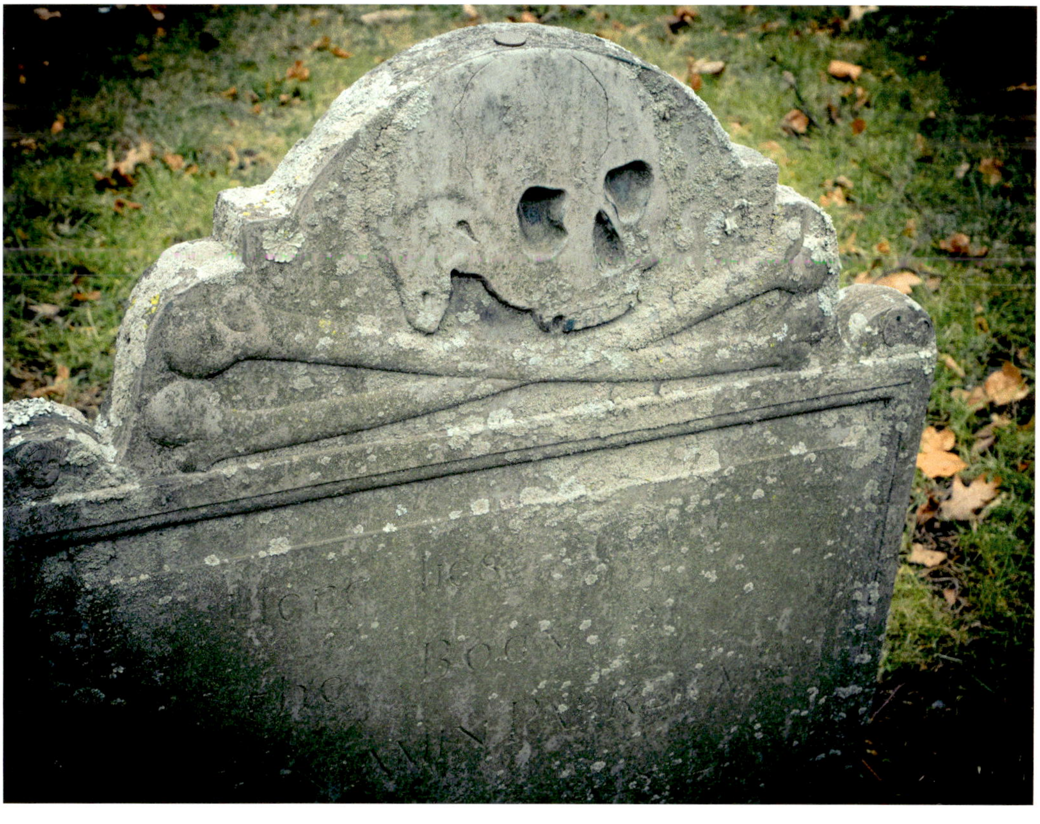

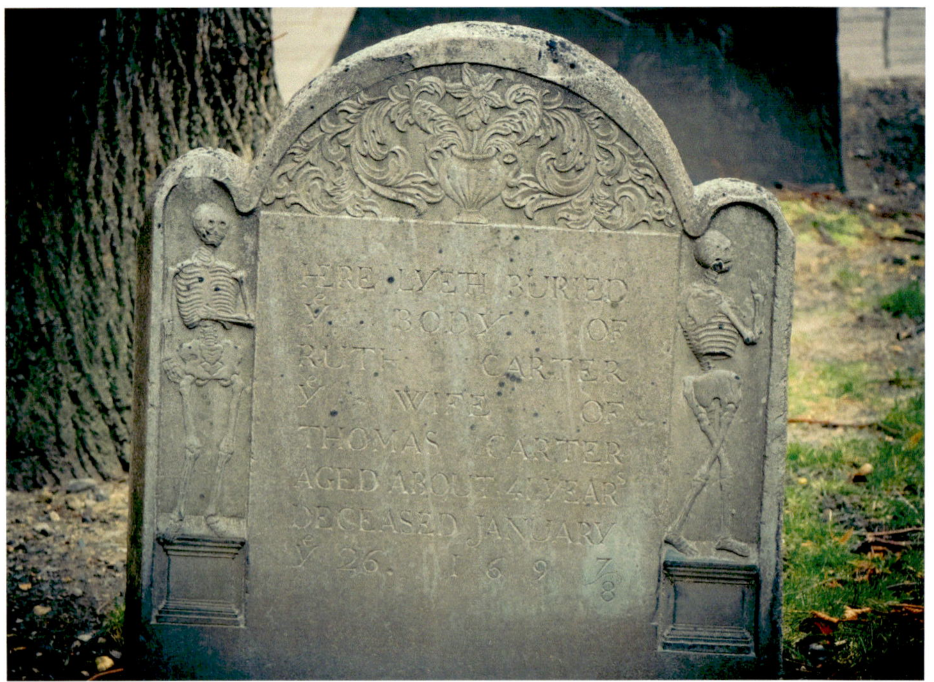

Skeltons flank the tombstone dedicated to Ruth Carter.

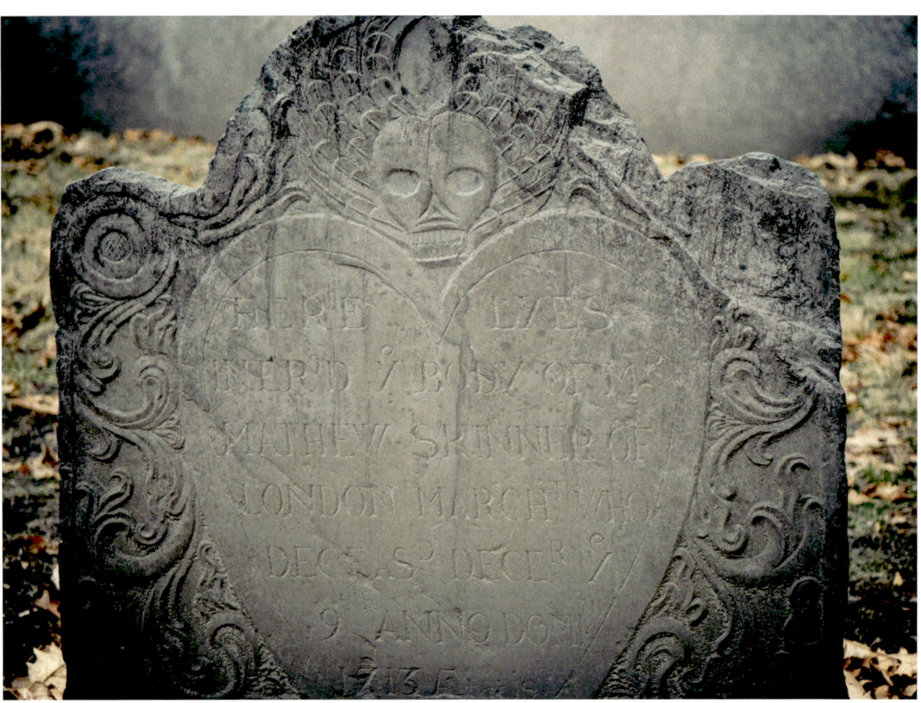

Hearts, a sign of love's triumph over death, can be seen on a few of the tombstones.

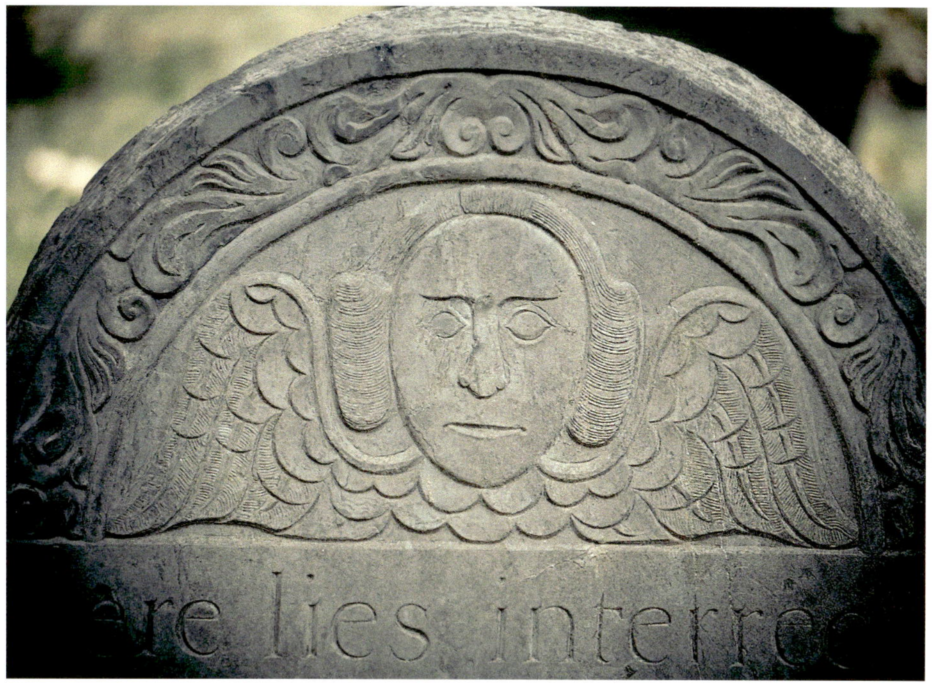

A cherub with a Colonial-inspired hairstyle.

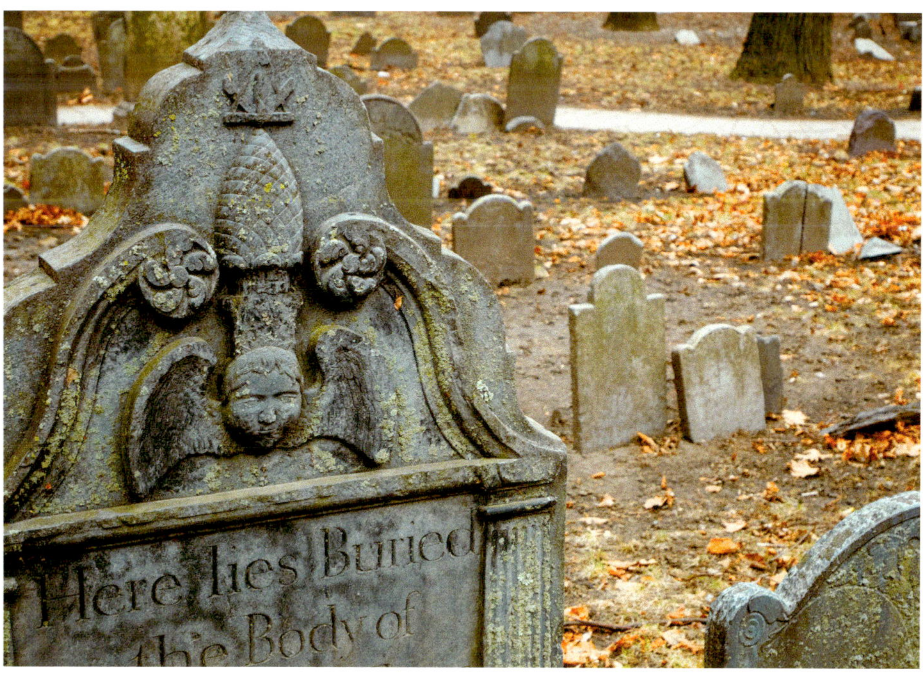

Despite being densely crowded, Granary Burying Ground still looks fairly organized thanks to the many rows.

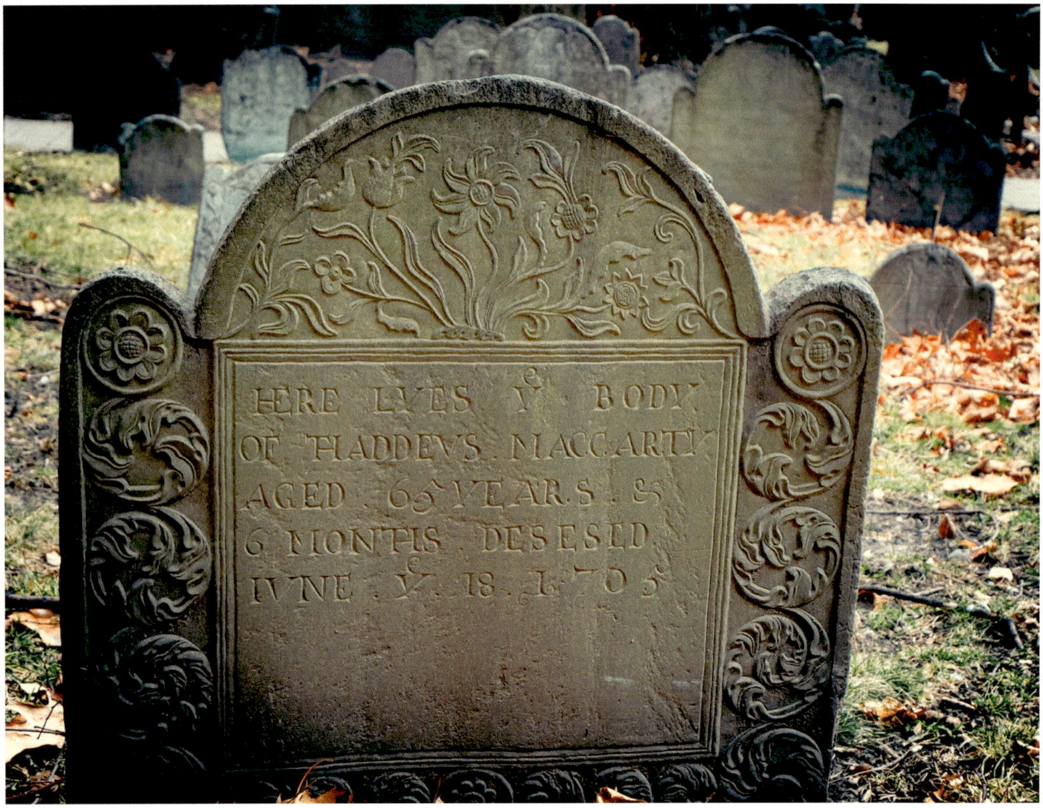

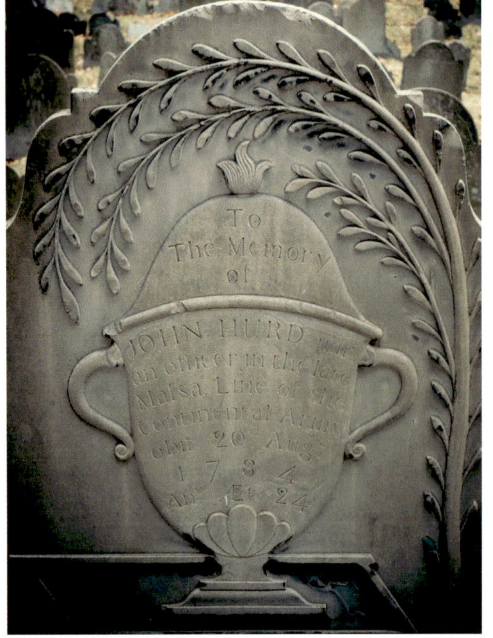

Above: A small garden can be seen sprouting from the ground on this tombstone.

Left: An urn and weeping willow are shown here in this vivid carving.

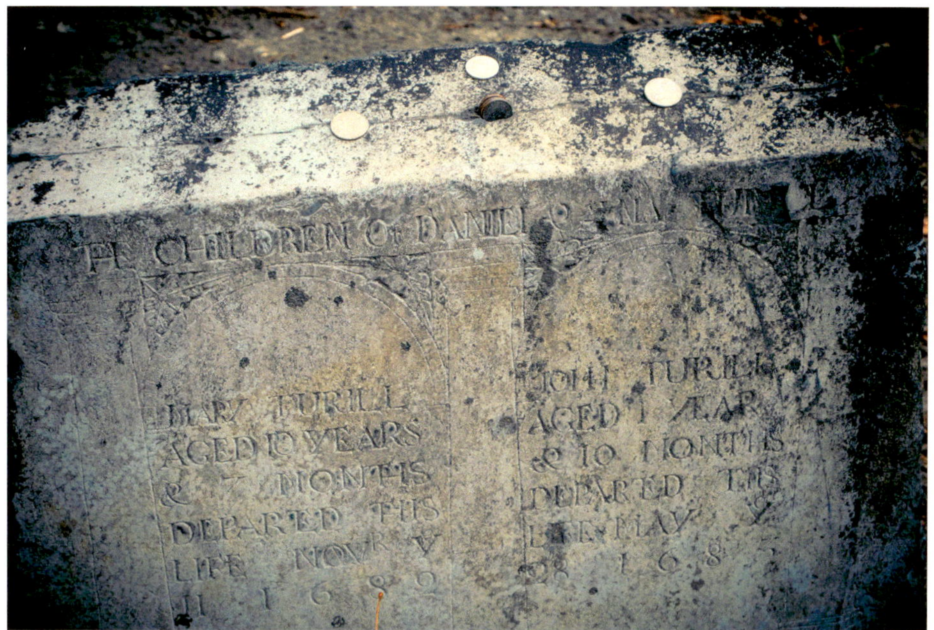

A stone dedicated to two lost children with a number of coin offerings.

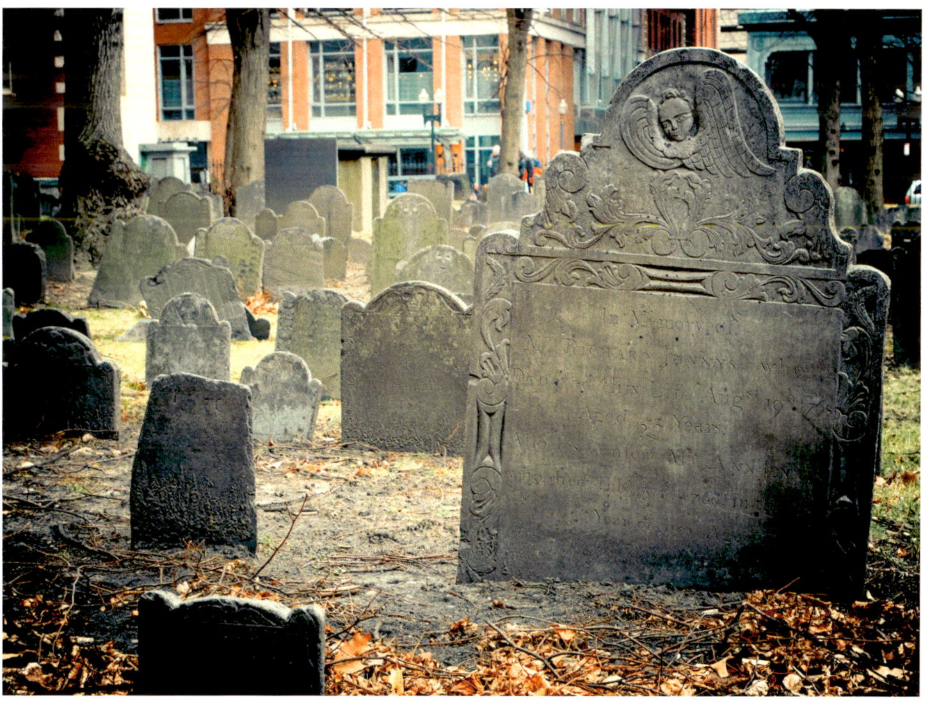

Granary Burying Ground is found on a bustling street right in the heart of the tourist area on the Freedom Trail.

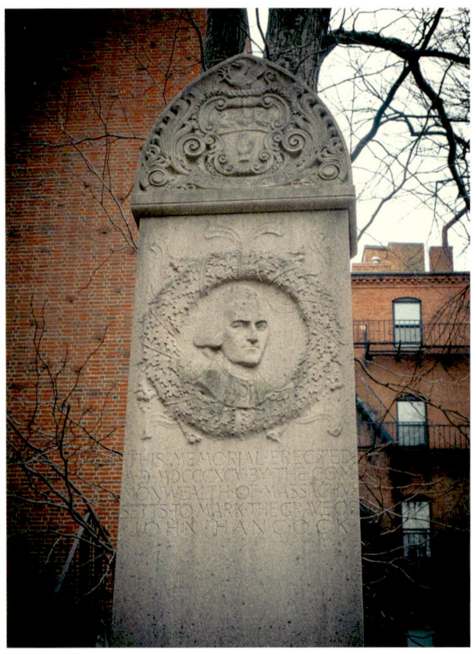

Left: Monument dedicated to John Hancock.

Below: An elaborate coat of arms on a family tomb.

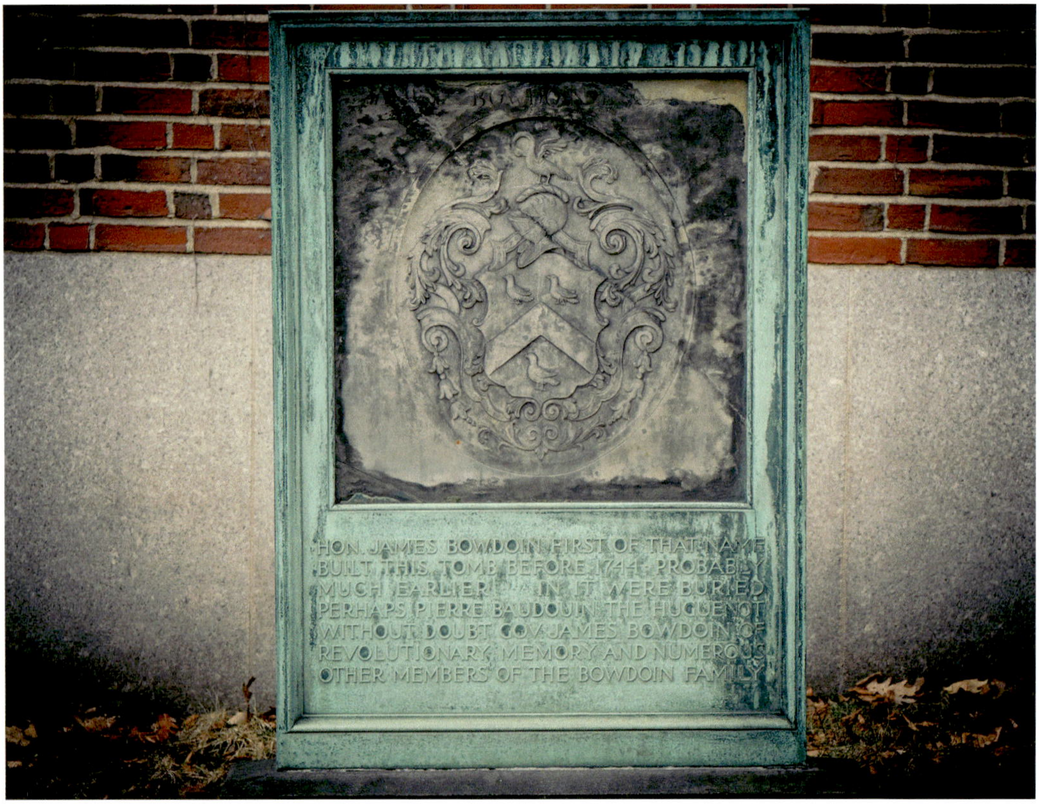

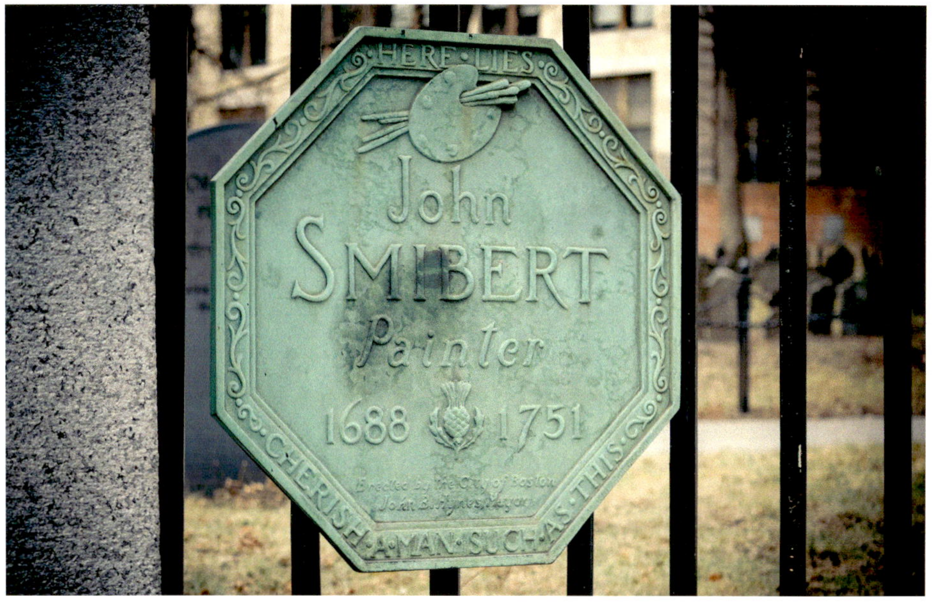

Plaque dedicated to the painter John Smibert, complete with paint brushes and palette.

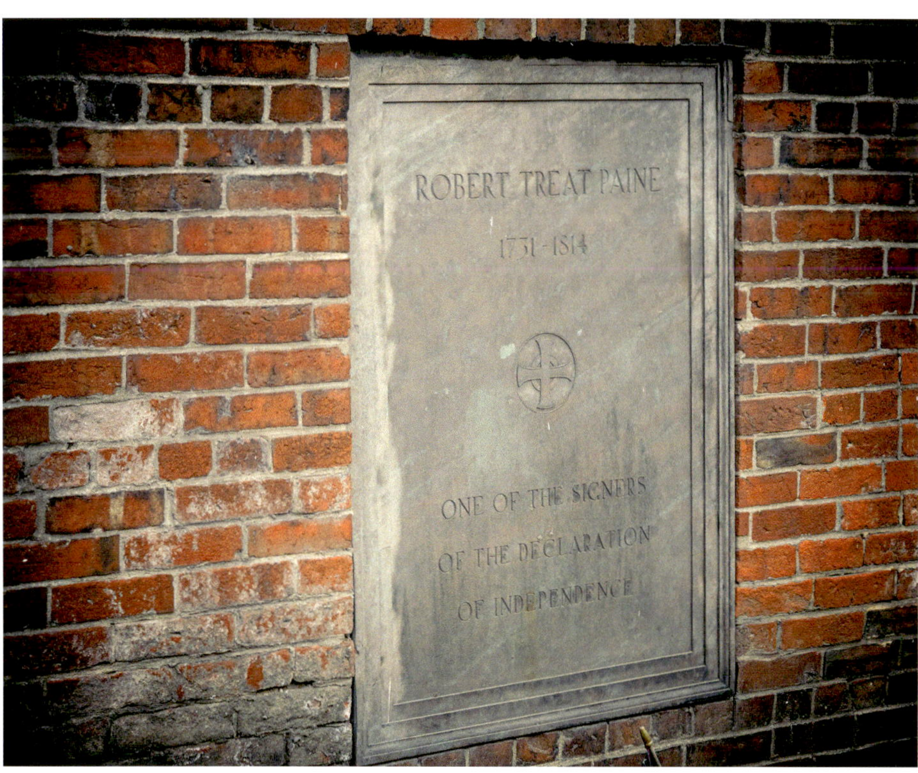

Tomb of Robert Treat Paine.

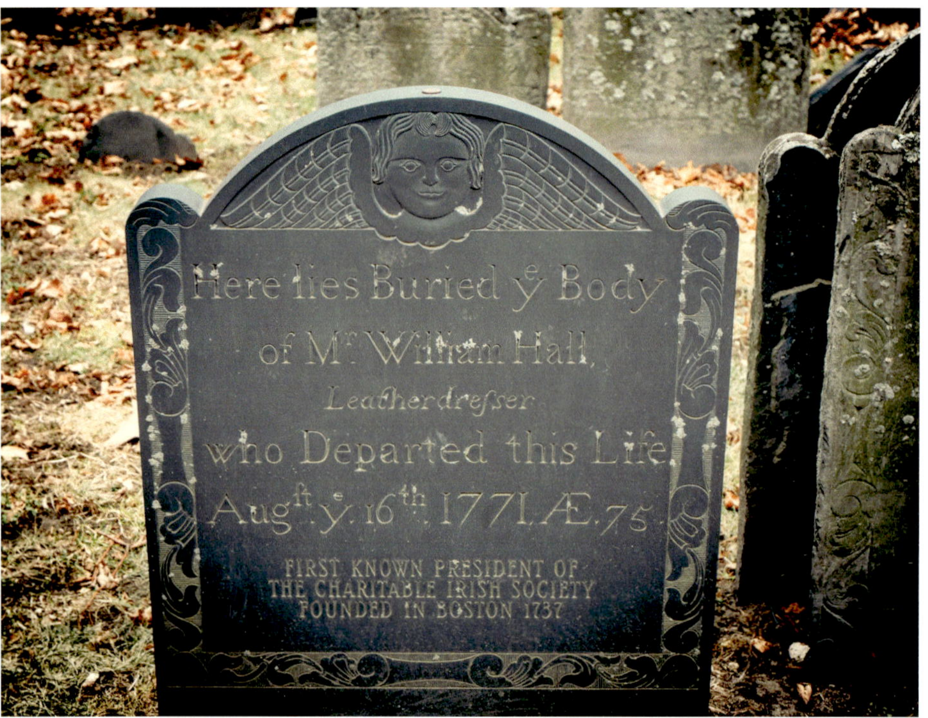

Memorial dedicated to William Hall, the first president of the Charitable Irish Society.

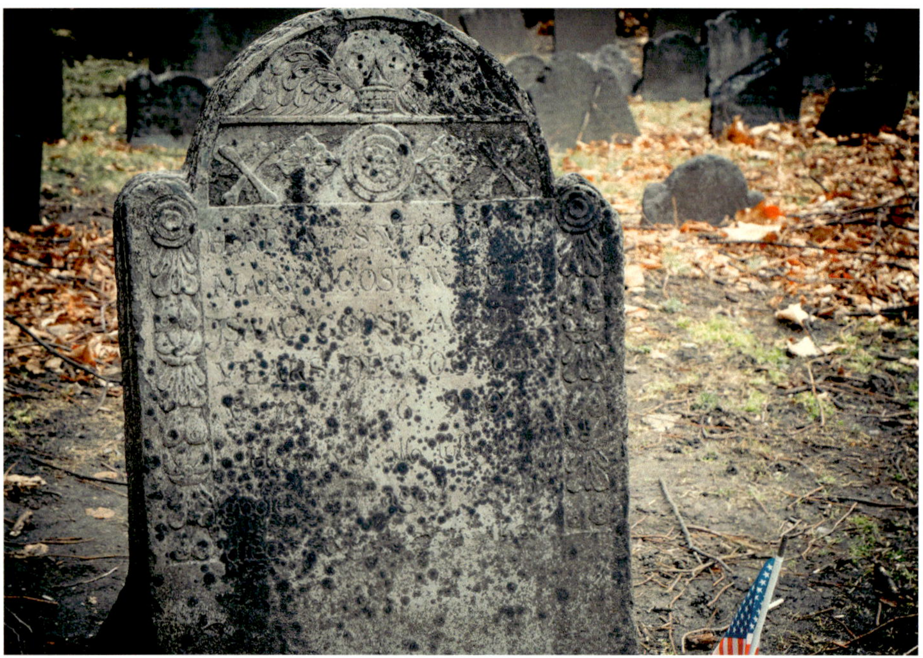

A favorite for tourists and selfies, this is the grave dedicated to Elizabeth "Mother" Goose.

6

Central Burying Ground

Directly across the way from the newly installed statue of famed writer, Edgar Allan Poe, is Central Burying Ground. Characterized by sporadically placed headstones, a lack of pathways, and limited shade, it is located on Boylston Street within the Boston Common.

Established in 1756, Central Burying Ground was desperately needed due to the substantial rise in population in Boston. The other three burying grounds (King's Chapel, Granary, and Copp's) had become vastly overcrowded as the result of increasing populations and numerous smallpox outbreaks in the 1720s. On March 10, 1740, a group of exhausted and overworked gravediggers created a petition saying that the other burying grounds had been so overpopulated that they "had to bury people four bodies deep and it was difficult to avoid disturbing previously buried corpses."[1] These desperate pleas would go unanswered until finally Central was established in 1756.

The Central Burying Ground has a rather distinctive history, as it has been forced to shift over the years as Boston expanded. In addition to almost constant new burials, there are also multiple people that have been reinterred here at Central from other burying grounds. Tombs were added to offer additional burial options around the 1800s. In 1804, multiple incidents were reported of interred bodies being wrongfully disturbed during new burials at both Copp's Hill and Central Burying Grounds. One gravedigger, it seems, had not been terribly concerned about where he was digging and left the previous remains out upon the ground. The gravedigger's only defense was that he was in too much of a hurry to find another spot since he had already started digging; he was subsequently fired from his job.[2]

Years later, Central Burying Ground had to contend with the construction of Boston's first subway system. The remaining tombs had to be removed, including any human remains that needed to be respectfully reinterred. The problem was that there were exponentially more bodies found than they had ever predicted—just over 800 to be precise.[3] These remains have now been reburied in a mass grave within Central Burying Ground, under a striking, contemporary stone that simply reads:

Here are the reinterred
the remains of persons
found under the Boylston Street Mall
during the digging of the subway
1895.

At the far end of Central is a fairly modern monument dedicated to the artist, Gilbert Stuart. Stuart, who died in 1828, is best known for his large-scale presidential portraits, including his famous paintings of George and Martha Washington. His monument is devoid of any *memento mori*; instead, a painter's palette has been carved on the stone.

It should also be noted that Central Burying Ground is home to an incredibly playful, thieving, and very large family of squirrels. During a fall afternoon, they can be seen jumping through the grounds and happily sitting on tombstones. Their determined goal is to seek treats from eager cemetery explorers that stroll through the burying grounds. The furry residents have no shame and will rifle through your bag if left unattended. I say this from personal experience.

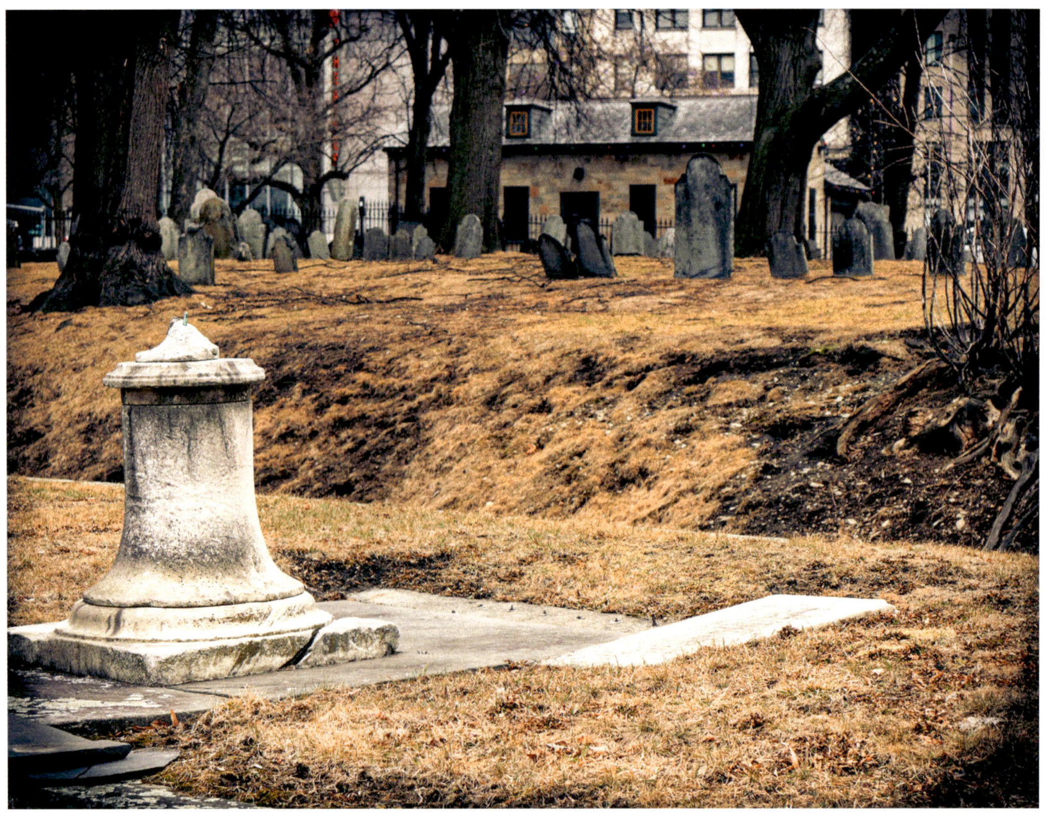

Central Burying Ground is found in the busy Boston Common.

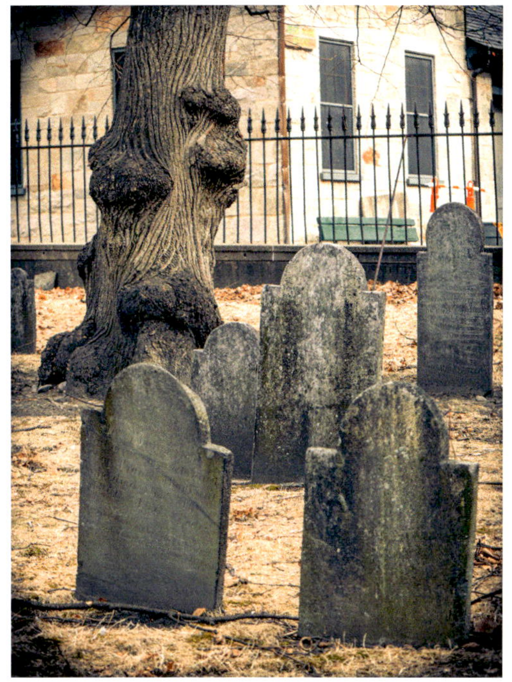

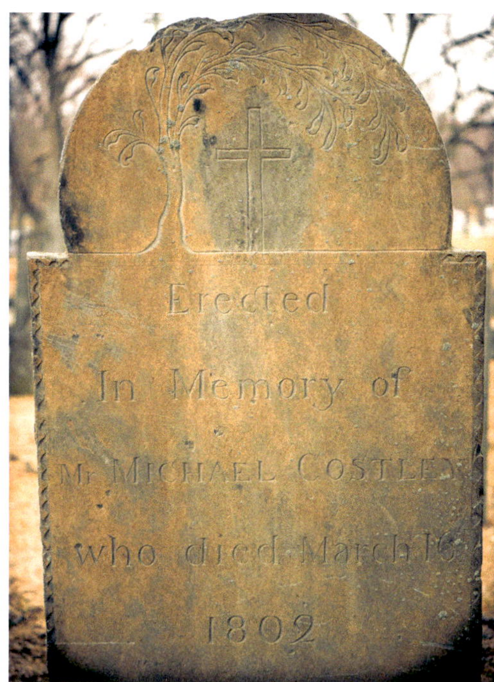

Above left: A sparse number of trees are found within Central Burying Ground.

Above right: A more modern stone with a simple weeping tree and cross.

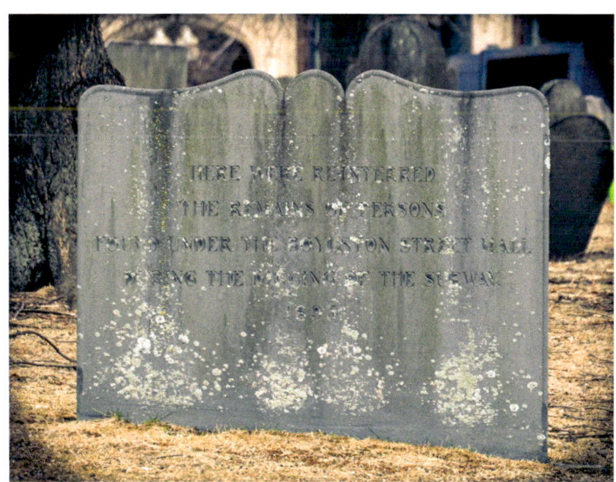

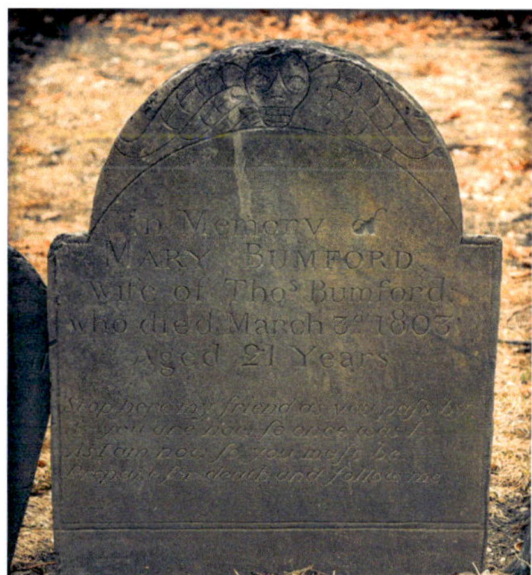

Above left: Memorial dedicated to those who were reinterred after the construction of the Boylston Street subway.

Above right: Monument dedicated to Marie Bamford, which reads, "Stop here my friend as you pass by, As you are now so once was I, As I am now so you must be, Prepare for death and follow me."

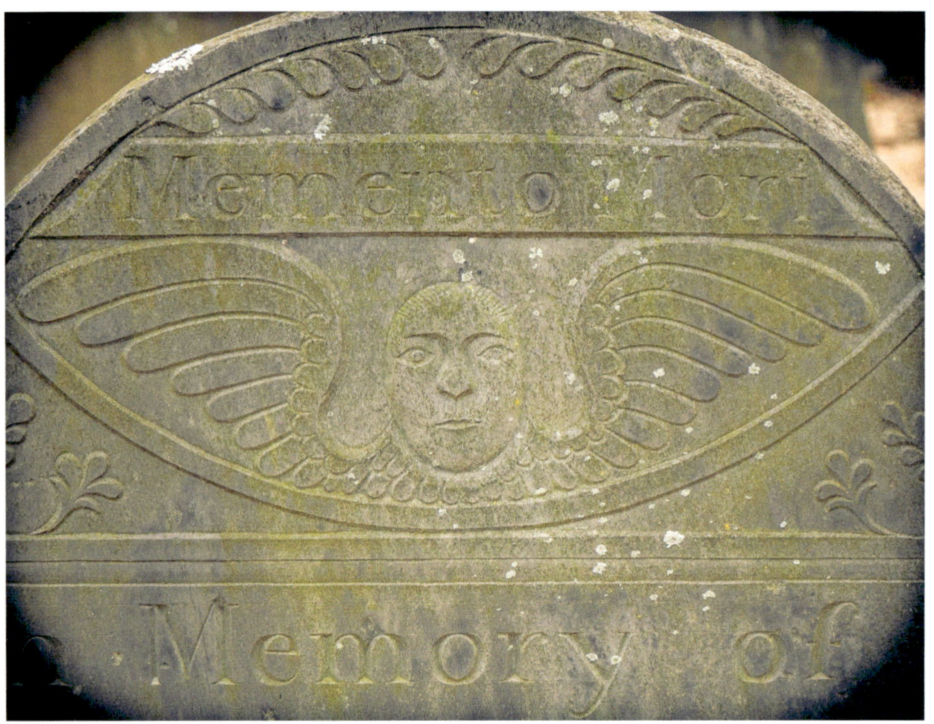

Stylized example of a cherub head motif.

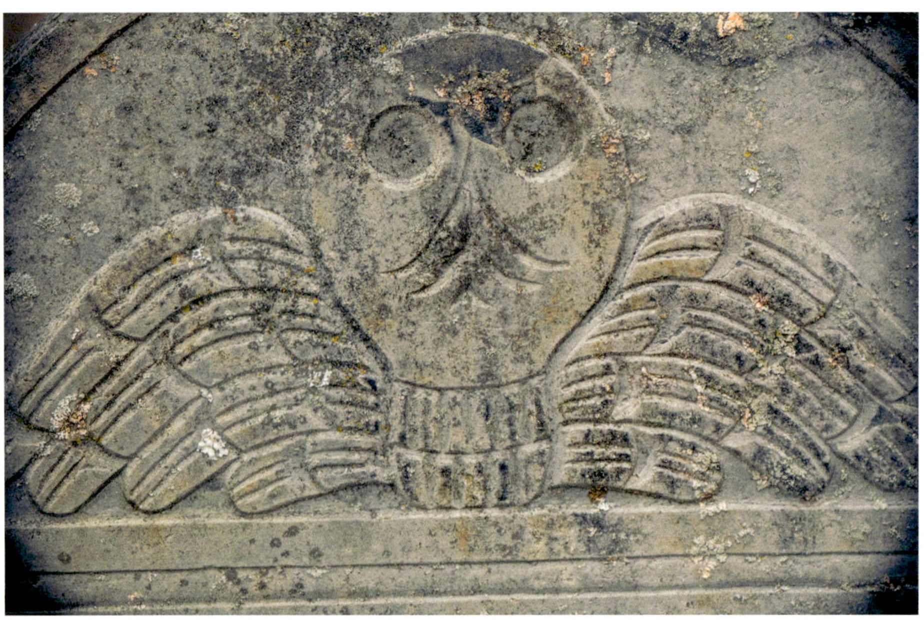

Some of the death's head designs are simplistic.

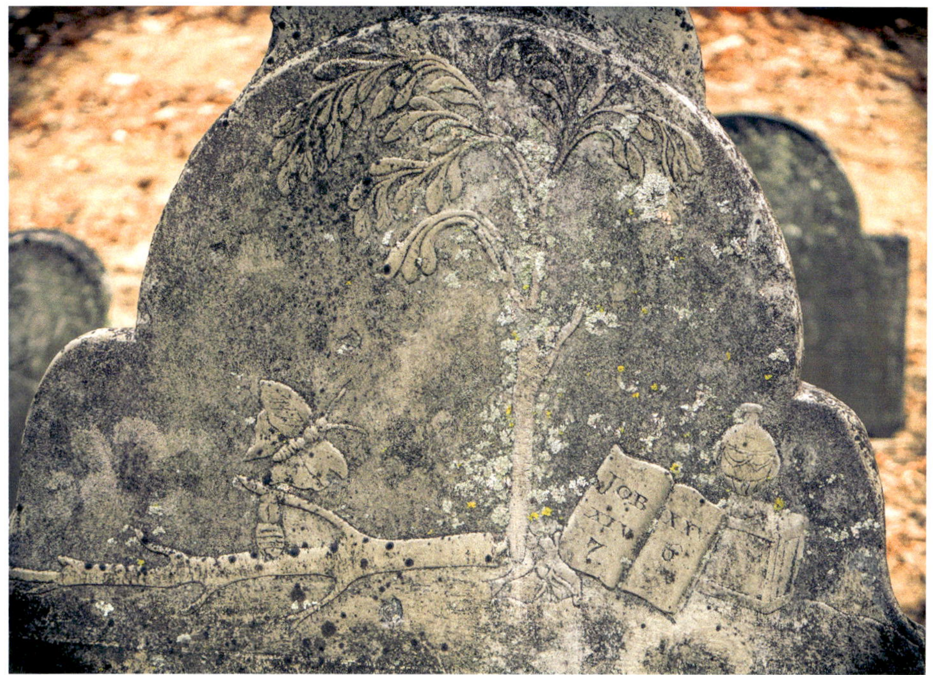

A much more elaborate tombstone than many of the ones at Central, this one features a butterfly and a fallen tree. The fallen tree is a symbol of a life ended, while the butterfly is a symbol of rebirth and resurrection.

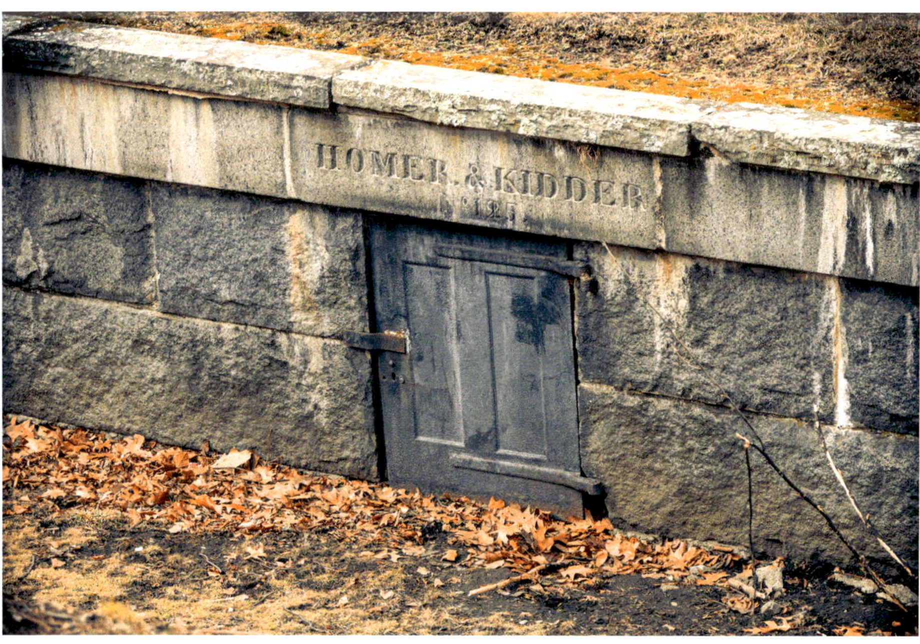

Underground tombs were also made available, like this one dedicated to Homer and Kidder.

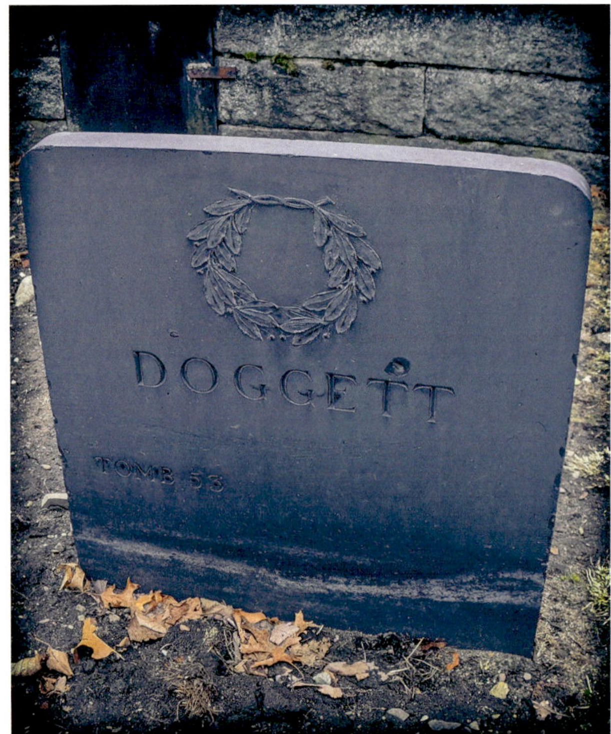

Left: A much more modern tombstone is dedicated to the Doggett family.

Below: The monument dedicated to Gilbert Stuart, famed portrait painter, is adorned with the painter's palette.

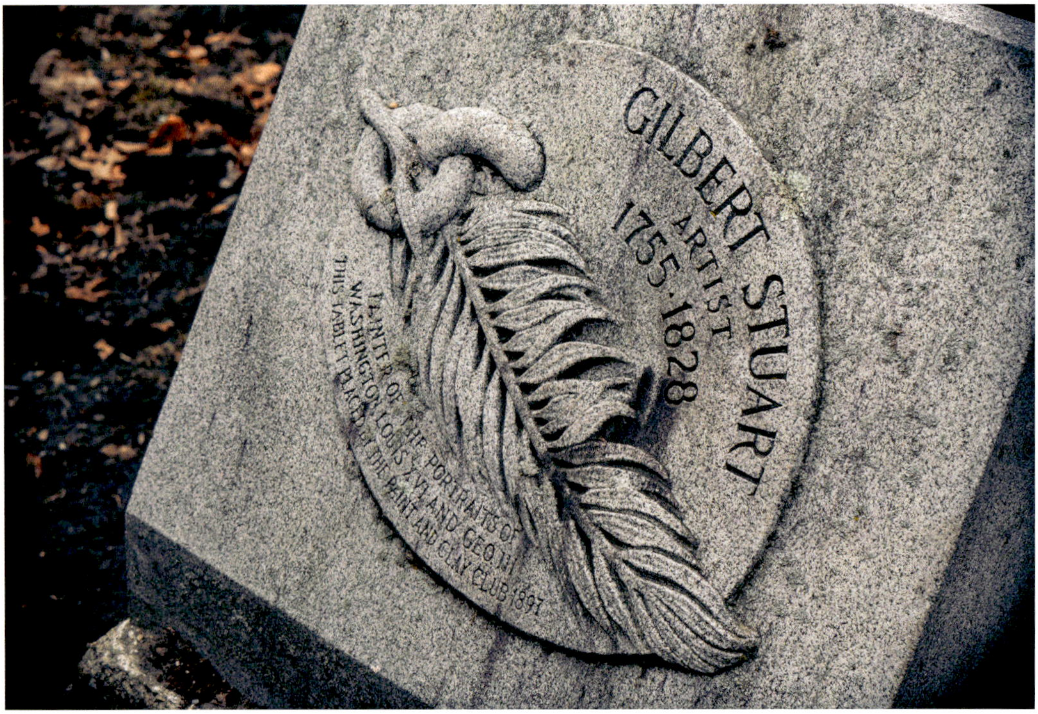

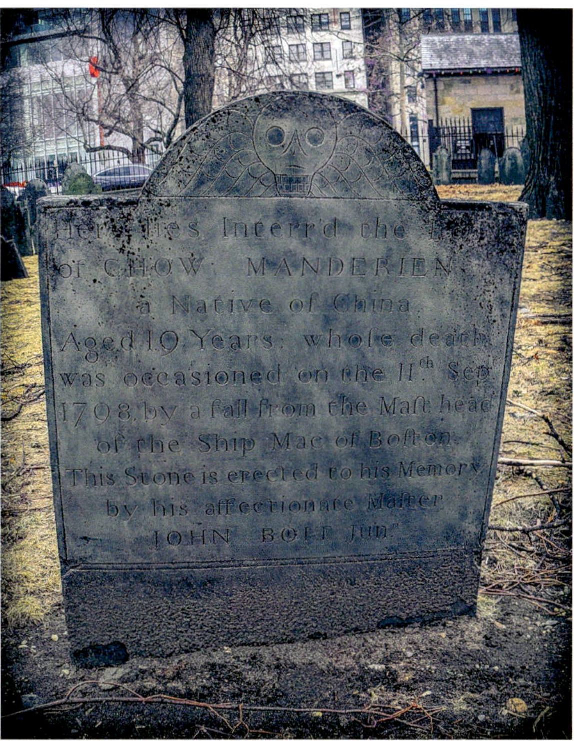

Right: The most interesting of all of the graves at Central Burying Ground is the one dedicated to a nineteen-year-old boy named Chow Manderien. He had fallen from the masthead of a ship on September 11, 1798. His death is the first known documentation of a Chinese person within the United States.

Below: The tombstones at Central Burying Ground are a variety of shapes and sizes.

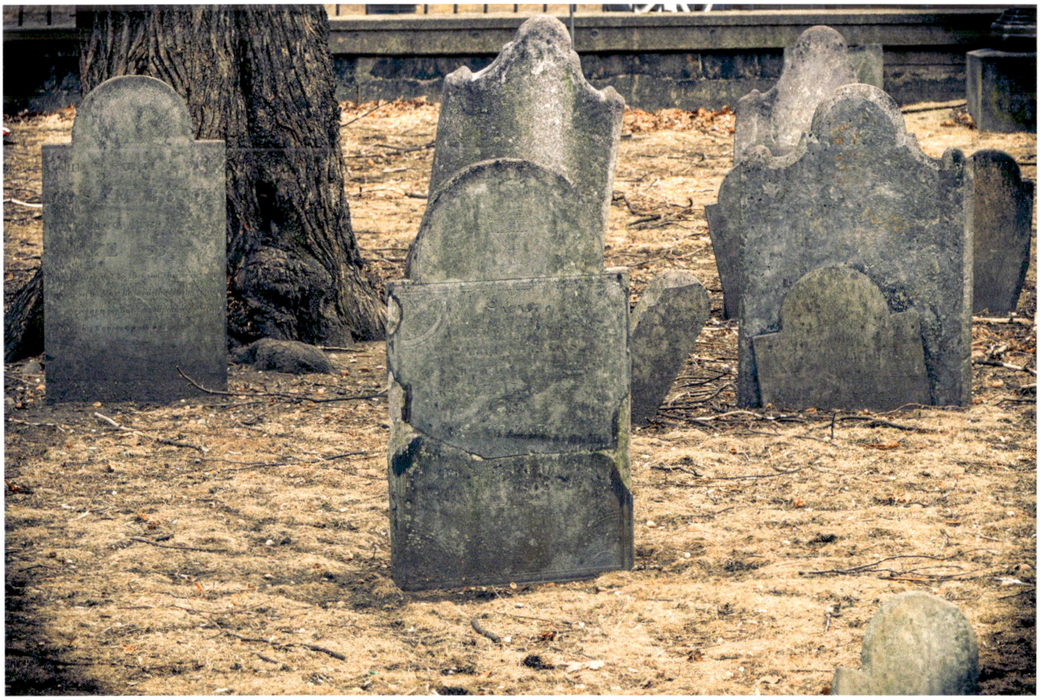

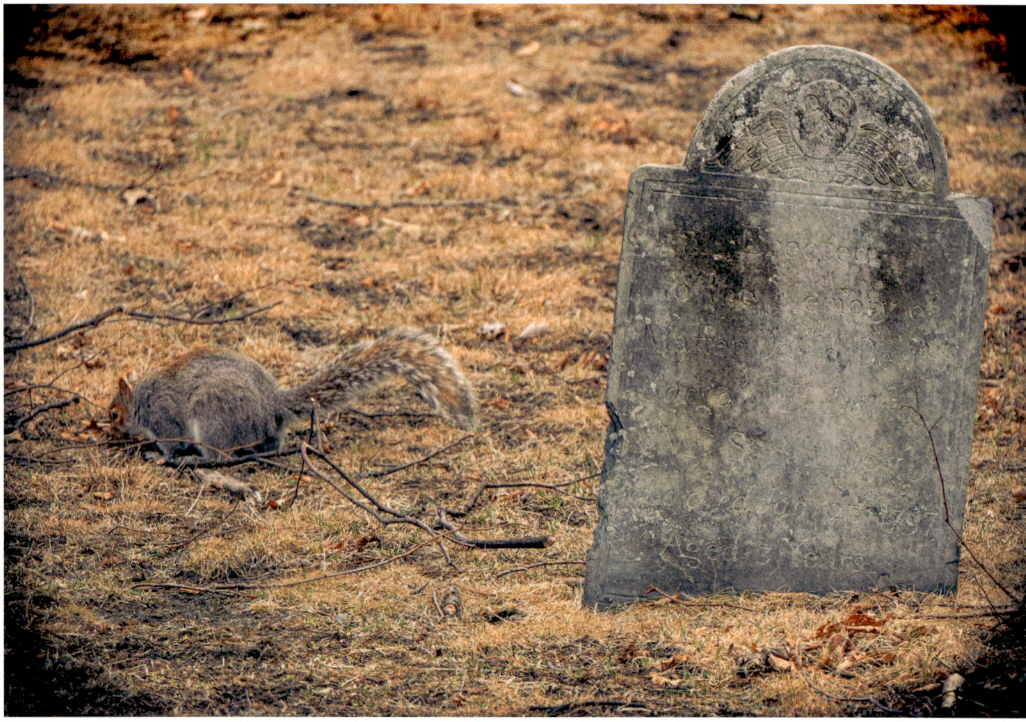

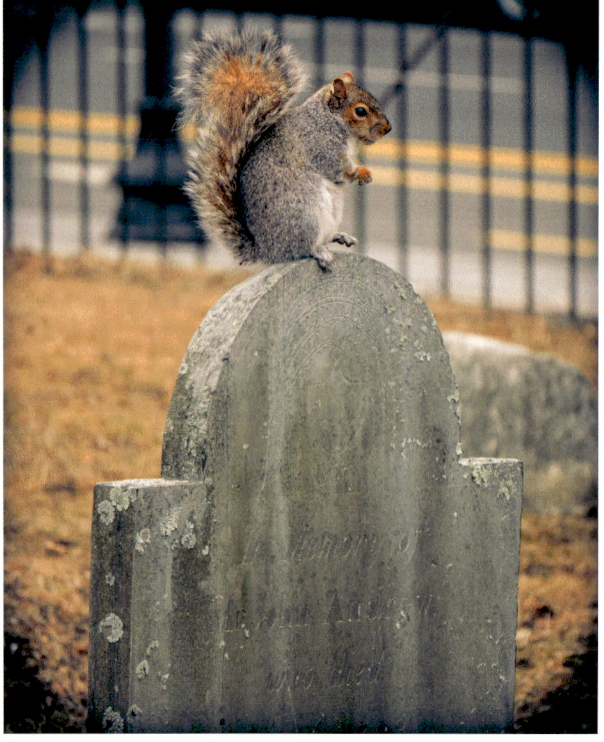

Above: These playful, furry friends are often very well fed due to the many tourists that come to visit the Boston Common.

Left: One of the many playful squirrel residents of Central Burying Ground.

7

MOUNT AUBURN CEMETERY

Just a short ride away from Boston proper is the illustrious and stunningly beautiful Mount Auburn Cemetery. While located in nearby Cambridge, this sprawling landscape cemetery is the direct result of the history of the burying grounds through the city of Boston. This cemetery is integral to Boston's history, as well as the history of rural cemeteries within the United States.

Up until the nineteenth century, there were few burial options aside from the church sanctioned burial grounds. The graveyards—like dozens found throughout Boston—were characterized by rows of nearly identical tombstones, with the larger monuments reserved for people of the upper class. These burial grounds, however necessary, were often dangerously unsafe and overcrowded. According to sources, "bits of old coffins and bones regularly turned up when new burials were made in common or family tombs."[1] As industrialization and urbanization drastically increased, so too did the city's population, and between 1861 and 1865 Boston's population had grown from 60,000 to more than 175,000 people.[2] This rapid increase in population meant not only accommodating the living but also raised the question of what to do with the city's numerous dead.

The city of Paris had already wrestled with the question of overcrowded graveyards and their unsanitary conditions for years. Their answer was to create the famous breathtaking garden cemetery that is Père Lachaise Cemetery. Père Lachaise designed in 1803, is located on 110 acres of land within the 20th arrondissement and was designed by Alexandre-Théodore Brongniart. Inspired by many lush English gardens filled with stunning trees, plants, and undulating pathways, Père Lachaise Cemetery would become a dramatic and much-needed shift away from the literal bone yards that many Parisian graveyards had become. It would become the final resting place of the deceased elite, known for its rich landscape, decadent monuments, and biodiversity. It would become world's first rural cemetery.

As American cities continued to grow, it became abundantly clear that they would have to address the issue of their deceased residents. With more people living in close proximity, the demand for burial space was rapidly on the rise. City officials and residents alike were forced to grapple with the challenge of finding a solution that

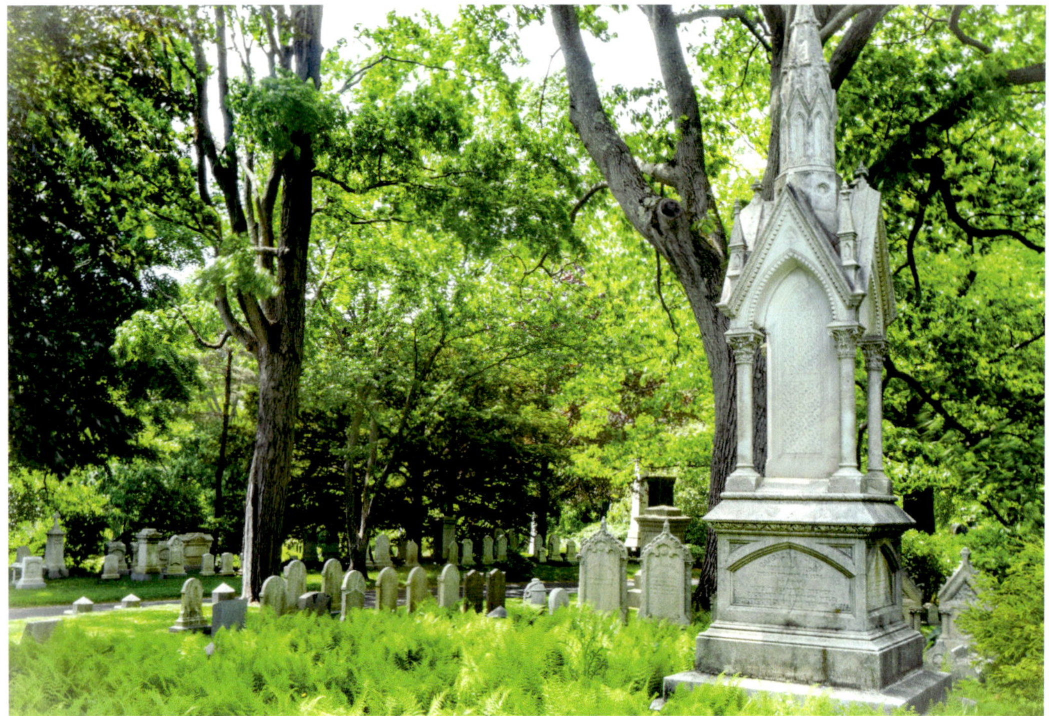

Mount Auburn Cemetery is filled with over 5,000 different types of plants and trees throughout 175 acres.

was both respectful and practical. The solution was the creation of an American rural cemetery, inspired by Père Lachaise. Much like its European predecessors, it would serve as a much needed and glorified location for the dead but would also offer a respite for living Bostonians to escape the confines of their dirty, overcrowded city.

At the same time, Americans also had a dramatic shift in their ideas about death. Infant and maternal mortality rates, as well as death from childhood illness, were on the rise. As a result of the Civil War, Americans would also find themselves constantly confronted by death on an overwhelming scale, as they dealt with the untimely death of over 750,000 people on their own soil.[3] It became imperative to find a solution to the growing dead.

While many church graveyards and burying grounds of the eighteenth century had admonitions of *memento mori*, a new sentimentality around death had become commonplace in America. The concept of the "good death" and the art of dying became regularly and openly discussed. American viewpoints regarding death, dying, and even mourning had drastically changed.

Death was now merely a step to the next life. The concept of a rural cemetery, much like Père Lachaise with a lush landscape, beautiful flowers, wandering roads, and lavish monuments dedicated to life, fit this new narrative. Instead of being a representation of impending and inevitable death, Americans leaned towards a cemetery with a greater focus on nature and the beauty of life. The answer was Mount Auburn, America's first rural cemetery.

Mount Auburn Cemetery was established in 1831. It would be the inspiration for many modern parks, as well as later rural cemeteries including the famous Green-Wood Cemetery in Brooklyn, New York, and Laurel Hill in Philadelphia, Pennsylvania. It is a sprawling 175-acre garden-style cemetery and arboretum just outside Boston in Cambridge, Massachusetts.

The cemetery was originally established on land known as Stone's Farm, but many of the locals commonly knew it as Sweet Auburn—in reference to the poem entitled *Deserted Village* by Oliver Goldsmith.[4] Mount Auburn Cemetery was designed as a result of the skills and dedication of the president of the Massachusetts Horticultural Society, Henry Alexander Scammell Dearborn; physician, Jacob Bigelow; and landscape architect, Alexander Wadsworth.

As of 2017, over 100,000 souls call Mount Auburn home.[5] The cemetery is filled with famous residents and historical figures, including Henry Wadsworth Longfellow, Isabella Stewart Gardner, and Winslow Homer. Other residents of note include author Thomas Bulfinch best known for *Bulfinch's Mythology*; reformer Dorothea Dix; and the founder of NAACP, Clement Morgan.

A visit to Mount Auburn can prove to be an extraordinary experience. Once past the towering spires of the chapel, you will be enraptured by the fragrant flowers that seem to exist at every turn. A quick walk past the main entrance, you can see countless green hills and trees which fill the expansive landscape. Thousands of unique monoliths cover the grounds. No longer are stones covered with winged skulls and sentiments of imminent doom, but instead, they express the idea of death as a transient stop. This sentiment is expressed perfectly on one grave that paraphrases a quote from James Aldritch's poem entitled *A Death Bed:*

> She passed through glory's golden gate, and walked in Paradise[6]

While the tombstones of Boston's burying grounds are unique in their similarities, the monuments of Mount Auburn are often incredible in their uniqueness. Deserted stone helmets and swords are seen on the graves of military men. Statues of weeping and mourning women are exceedingly popular. Dozens of flawlessly carved angels with their outstretched wings are found throughout the grounds.

The gravestones and memorials of Mount Auburn include personal details of the life of the deceased, no matter how brief. The grave dedicated to Mary Wigglesworth is particularly poignant. Having died before she was even one year old, her stone memorial is an abandoned and empty baby's bassinet. The empty bassinet signifies a baby who never got to live, as evidenced by the bassinet she would never sleep in again.

Well worth the trip and a full day to explore, Mount Auburn Cemetery marks a distinctive change in the history of American burials. Its beautiful landscape resounds as a perfect example of the new American viewpoint towards the art of death. The result is a cemetery that is not only functional for its permanent residents, but an astonishingly beautiful place for living visitors as well.

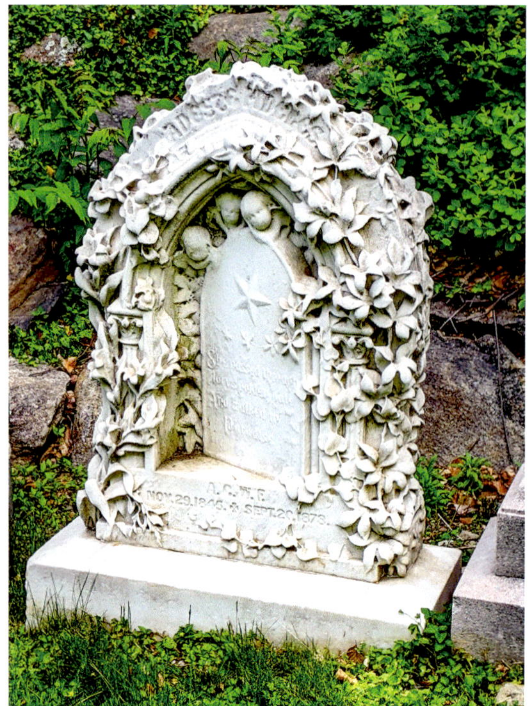

Left: In addition to a quote from James Aldrich's poem entitled "A Death Bed," this stone also has several small souls moving through a door to the next life and is adorned with dozens of hand-carved flowers.

Below: The stone bassinet of Mary Wigglesworth.

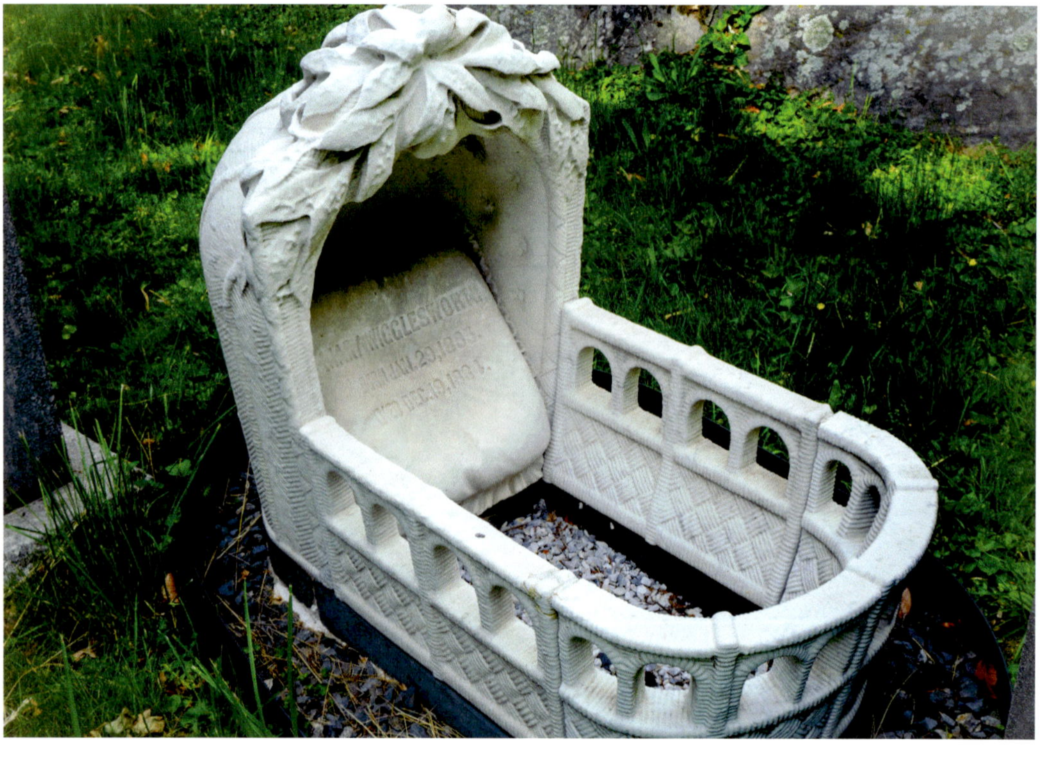

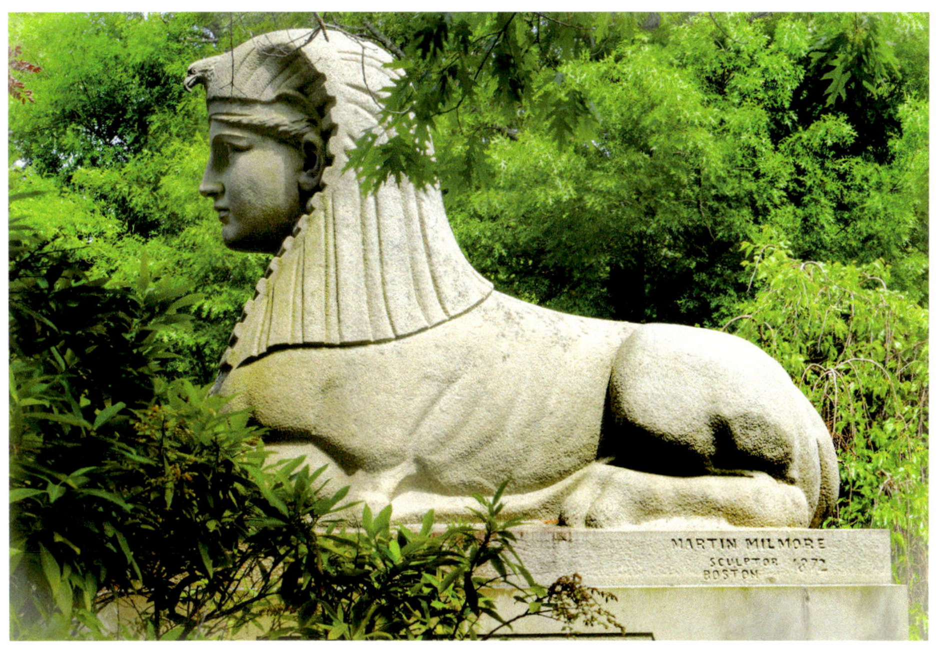

The Milmore Sphinx serves as a memorial to the Union casualties of the Civil War.

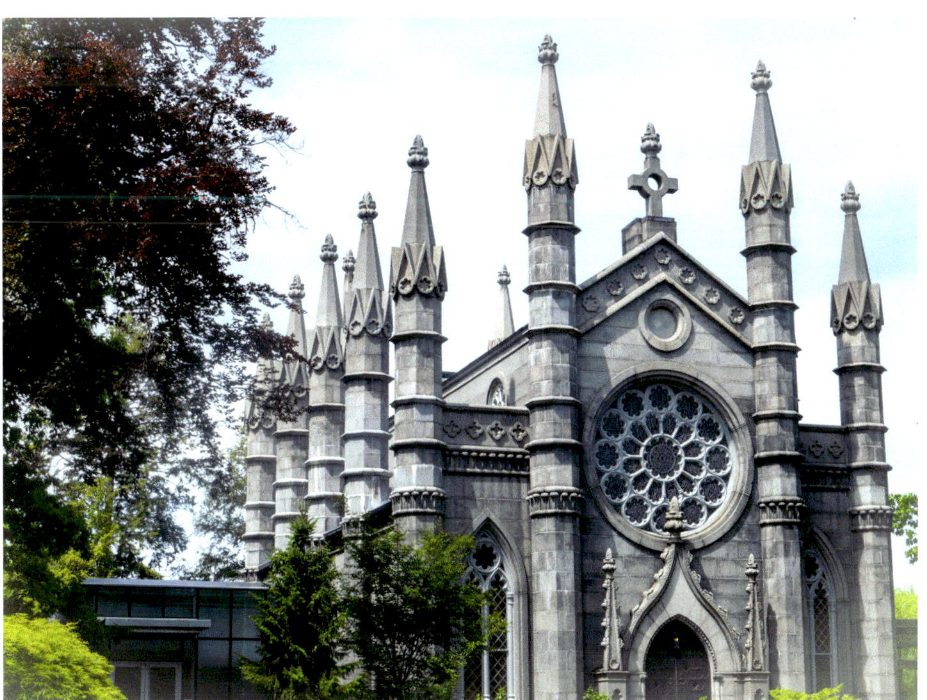

The Mount Auburn Chapel.

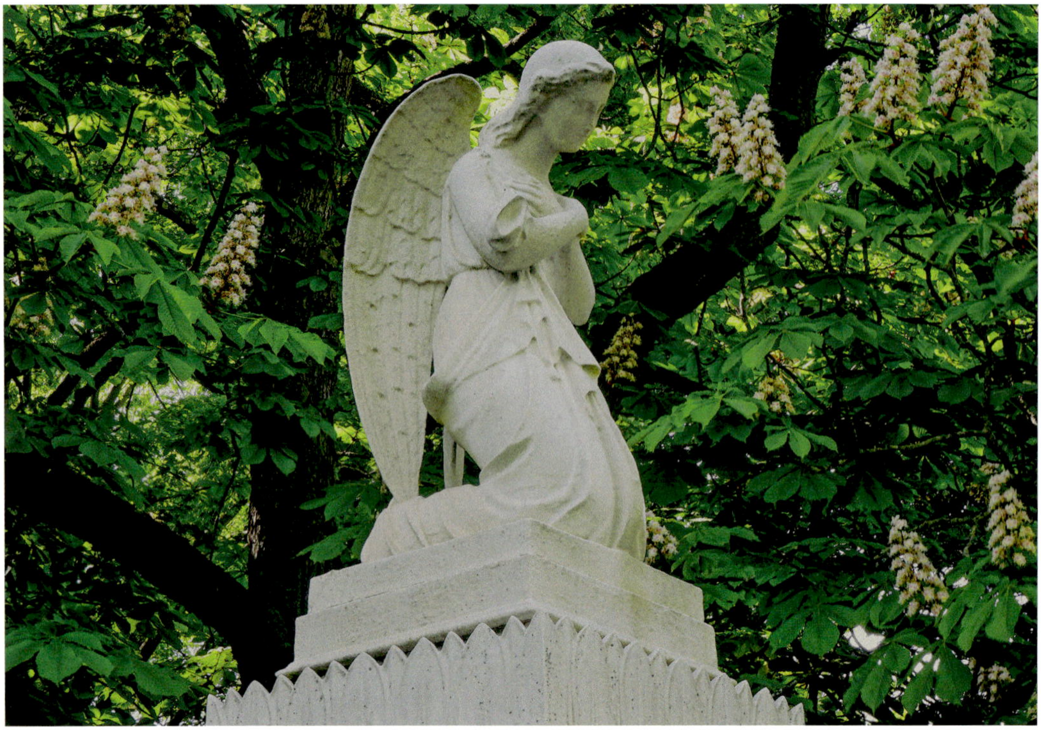

One of many angels in prayer found throughout the grounds.

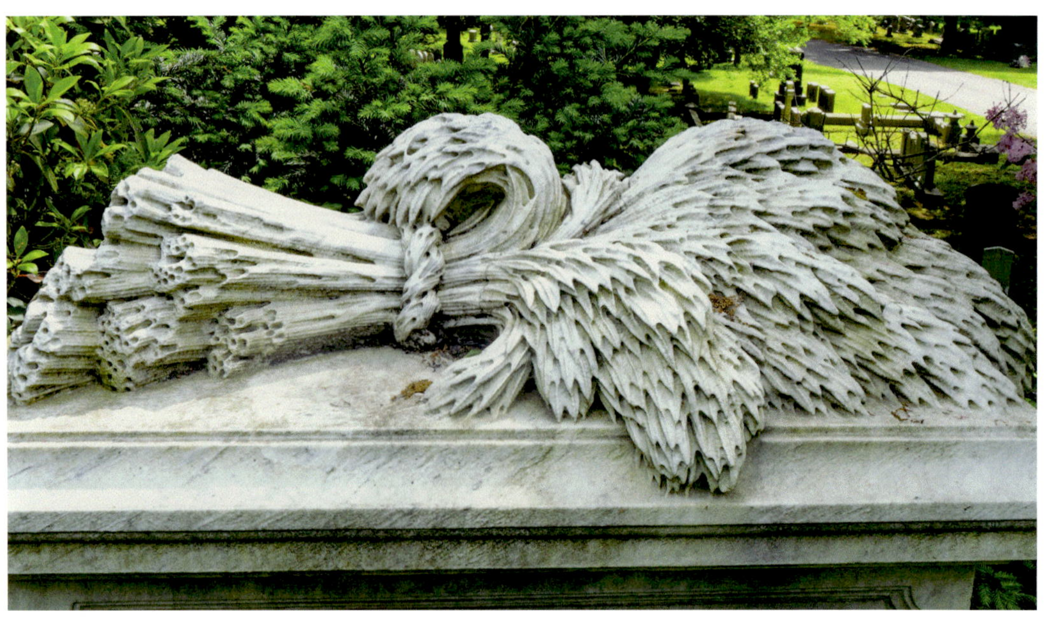

A sheaf of wheat is a symbol of a long and prosperous life, usually found on the graves of individuals who passed at an old age.

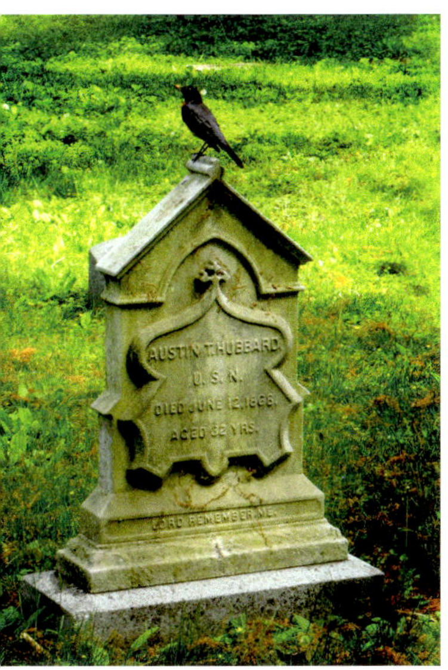

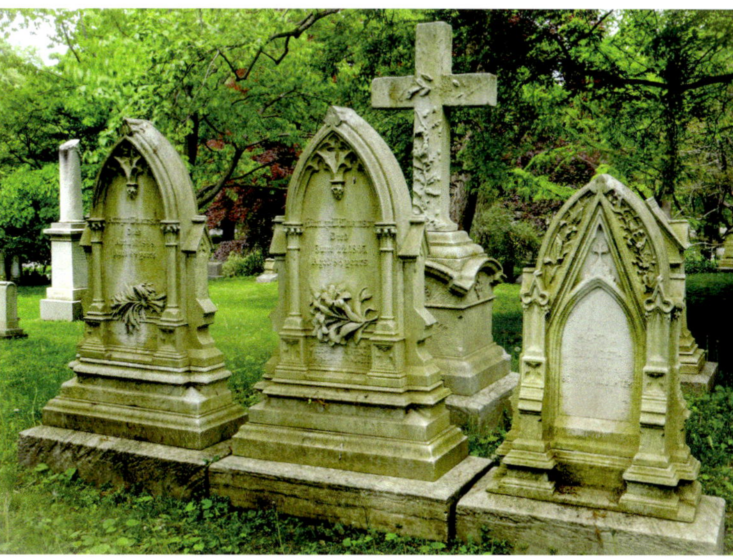

Above left: Mount Auburn is also home to many birds and small animals.

Above right: Many of the gravestones are adorned with carved flowers and plants.

Below: In the rural cemetery, death's heads are a thing of the past. Instead, you will find many angels with outstretched wings or hands clasped in prayer.

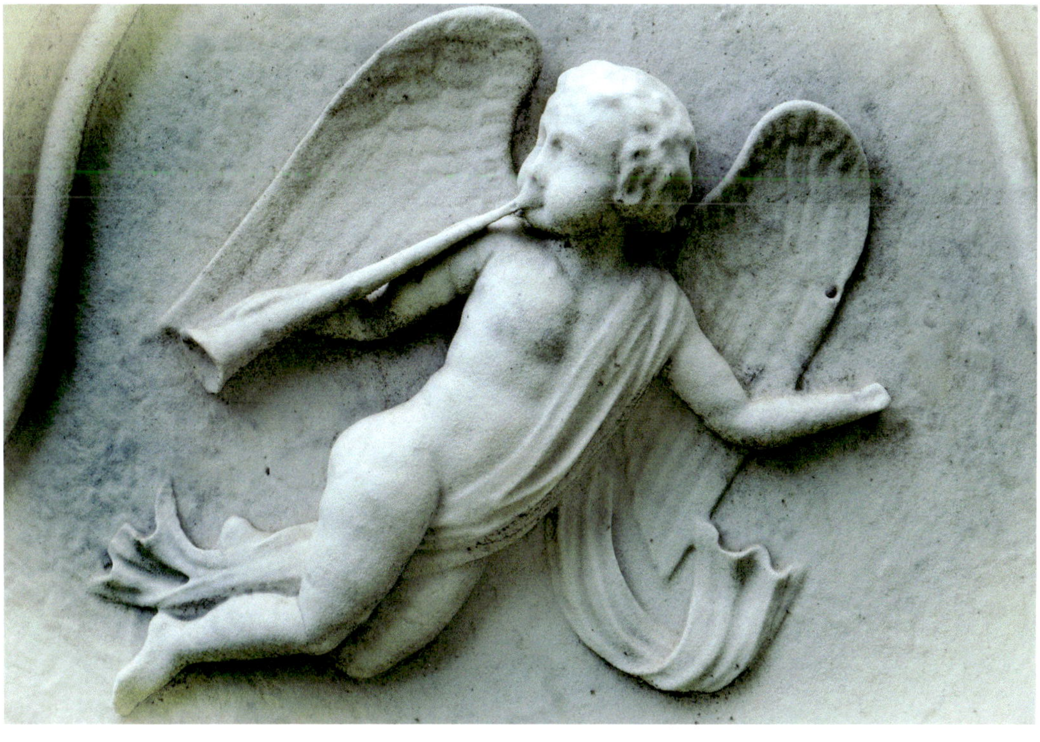

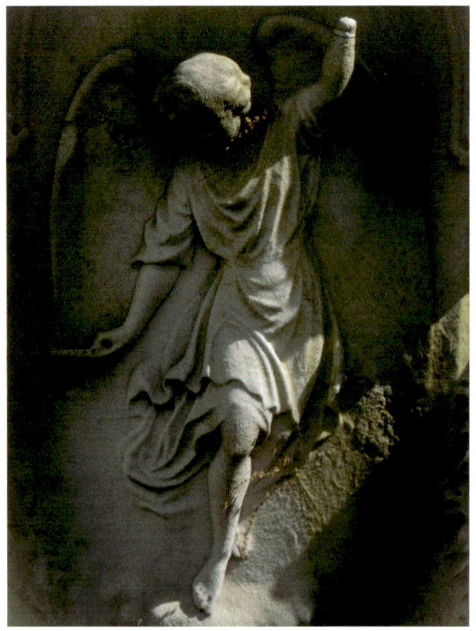

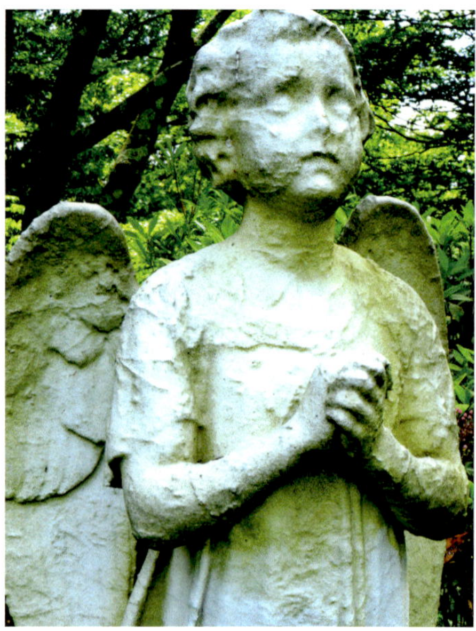

Above left: Another fabulous angel of Mount Auburn, this one can be seen stepping on a small carved cloud.

Above right: A number of angel statues have round, childlike faces with large eyes and a gentle curl to their hair.

Below left: An upside-down torch with the flame still burning is a symbol that life may have ended, but the soul remains eternal.

Below right: Monument of a child tightly holding a book.

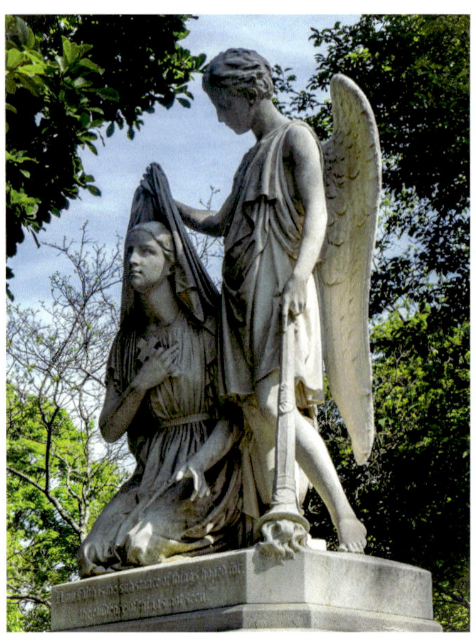

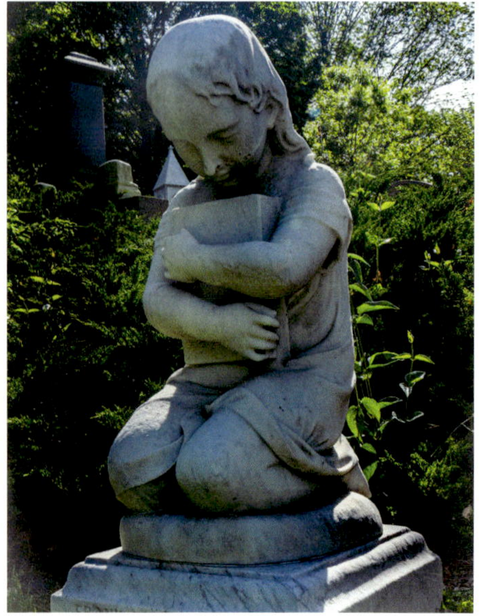

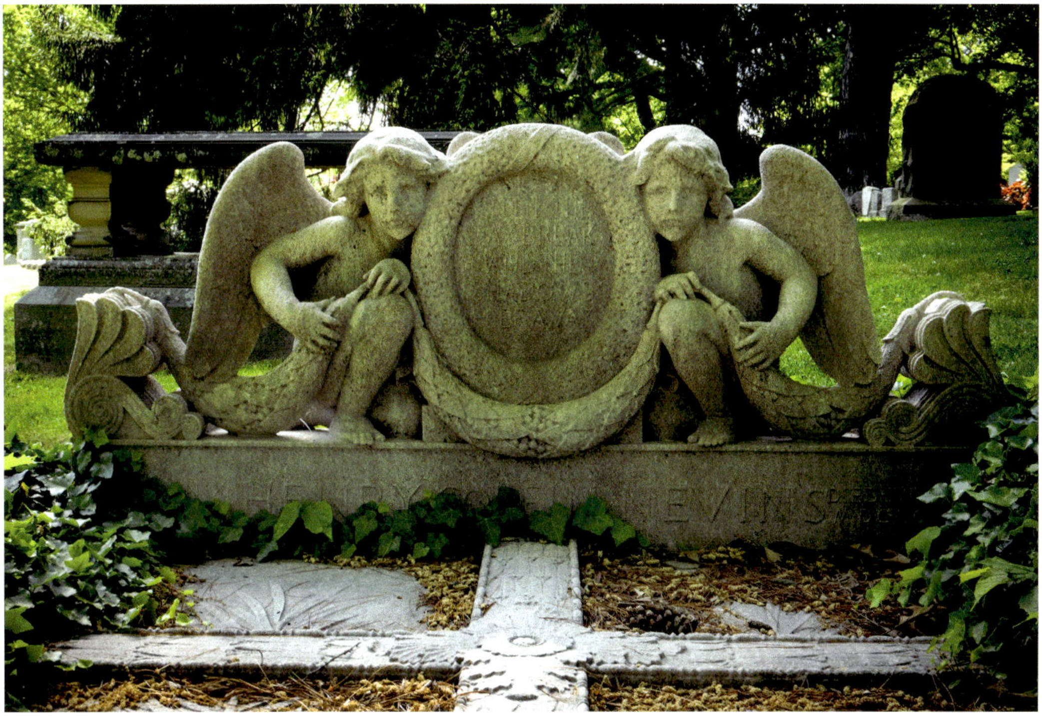

Above: Two watchful young angels guard an ivy covered grave.

Right: The voluminous carved flowers double as permanent bouquets.

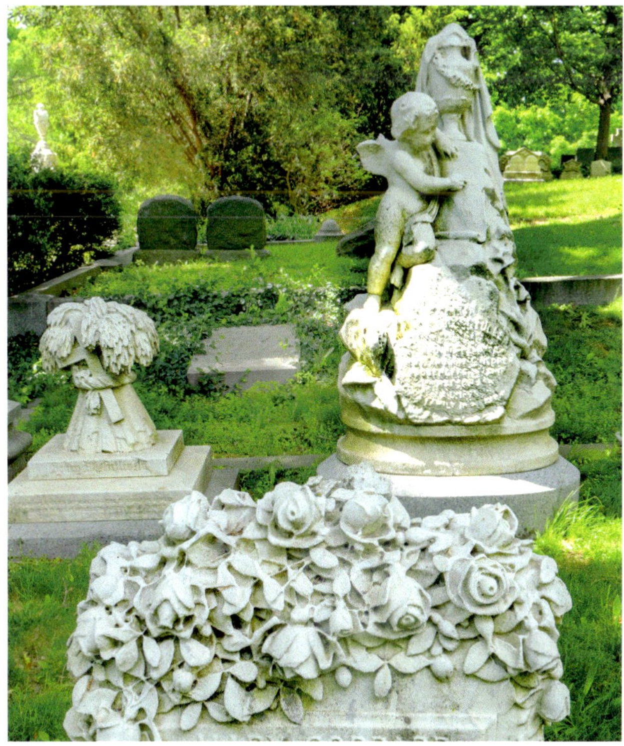

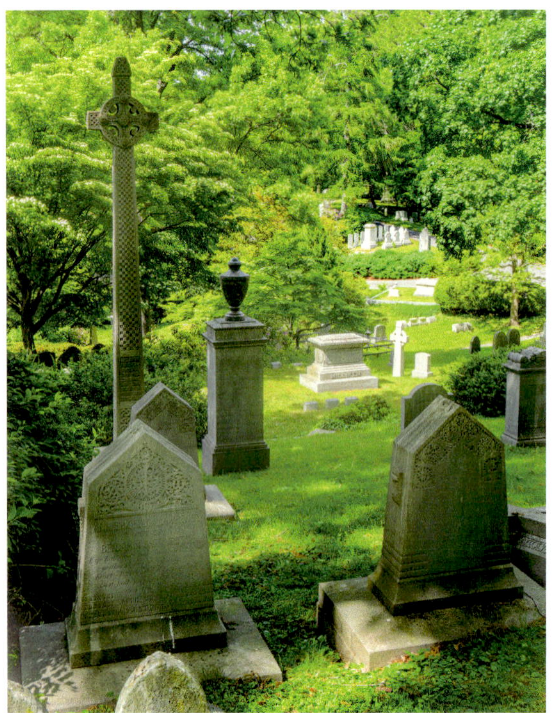

Left: Mount Auburn is filled with rolling hills, beautiful vistas, and a stunning green landscape.

Below: Some statues are hard to find amidst the rich vegetation.

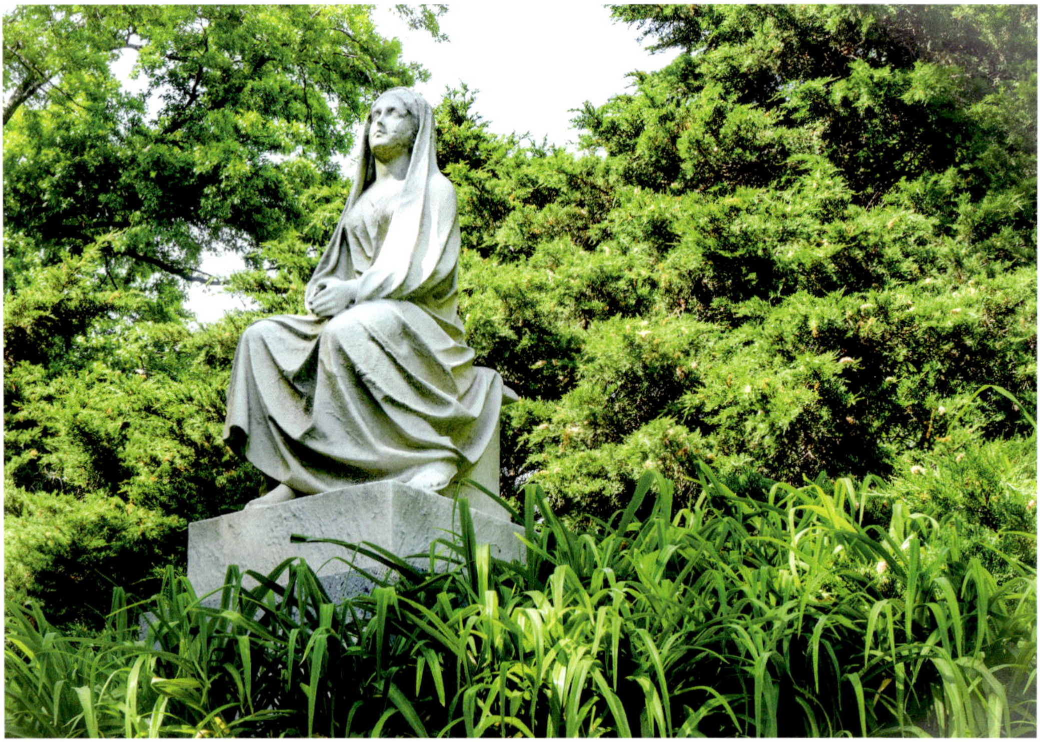

8

FOREST HILLS CEMETERY

Established in 1848 and designed by Henry A. S. Dearborn, Forest Hills was created as a park-like setting for friends and family.[1] While stunning in its own right, Forest Hills is perhaps most known for the many famous people buried here, including E. E. Cummings and Eugene O'Neil.

To the immediate left of the cemetery's Gothic Revival-style gate is Daniel Chester French's *Martin Milmore Memorial,* otherwise known as *Death and the Sculptor.* The bronze memorial shows a sculptor as he diligently chisels away on a sphinx monument, his hands guided by a towering Angel of Death. The Angel of Death appears as if she is about to actively step out of the sculpture in front of us. In her hands is a small bouquet of poppies, symbolizing eternal sleep. The relief statue was described as "one of the finest pieces of outdoor art in the nation."[2] *Death and the Sculptor* was originally commissioned by the family of the sculptor, Martin Milmore (1844–1883), and his brother, Joseph (1841–1886), to memorialize their life and their work.[3] Underneath the mammoth statue is a plaque that reads:

> "Come Stay Your Hand," Death to the Sculptor Cried,
> "Those who are sleeping have not really died."

This statue not only serves as a striking introduction to the fascinating sculpture garden of Forest Hills Cemetery, but it also shows a creative link with Mount Auburn. The sphinx within the monument is a reference to the Milmore Sphinx that greets visitors outside the Mount Auburn Chapel. A marble version of the work also exists in the galleries at the Metropolitan Museum of Art in New York City.

In a cemetery already filled with amazingly poignant art, some of the most breathtaking and haunting memorials involve children. The death of a child is always a life-altering and painful experience which was a common occurrence at the time. The monuments dedicated to such deep losses are personal, intimate, and eternal signs of a parent's extreme grief. Two such examples are the life-sized statues of Grace and Louis, both of whom died before seven years of age. They are hauntingly life-like, extravagantly detailed, and permanently encased in glass.

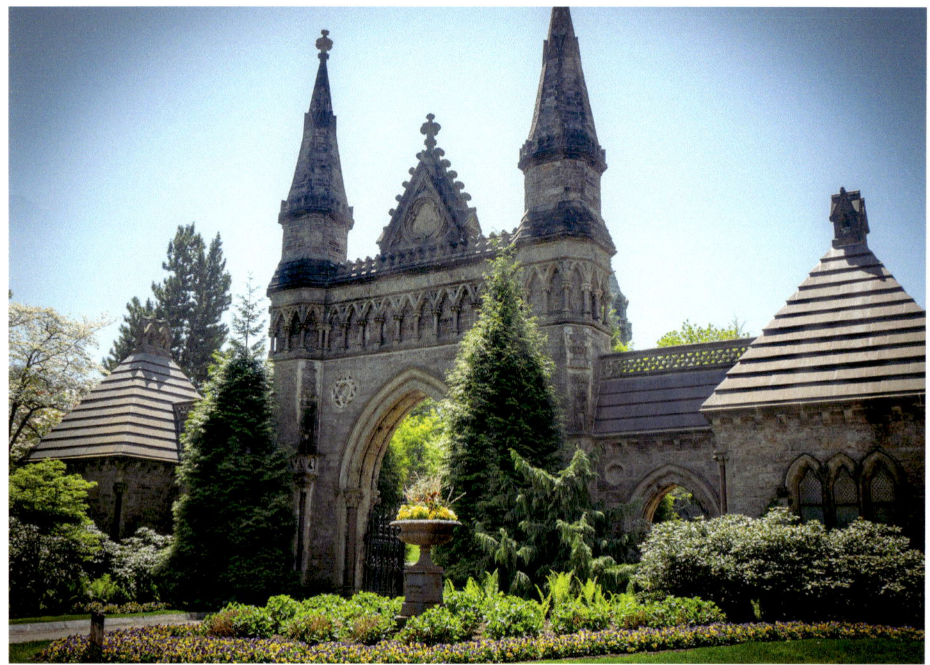

The gorgeous Gothic Revival entranceway of Forest Hills Cemetery.

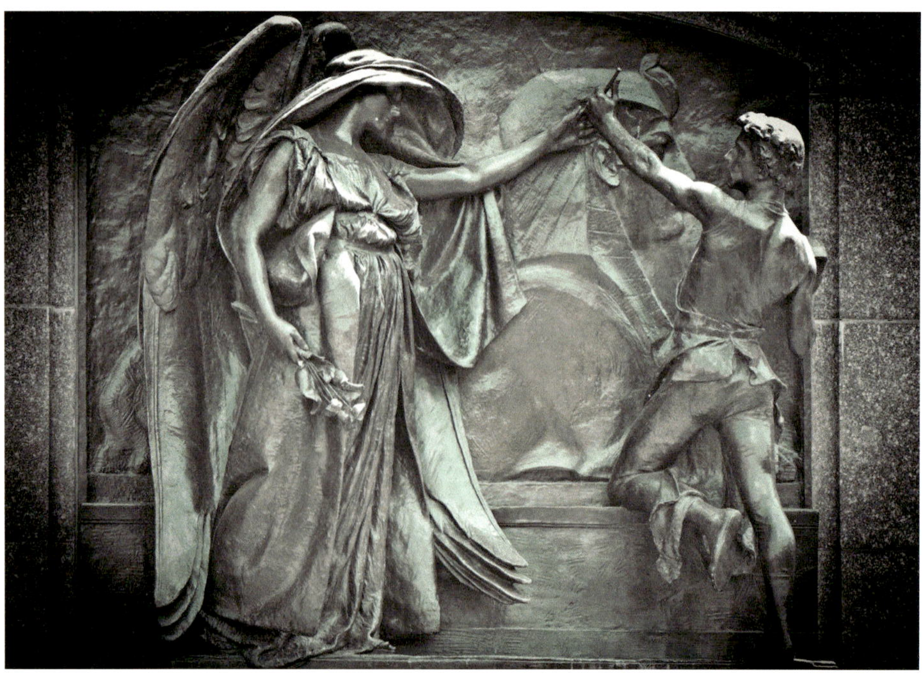

The image of death had clearly changed by the Victorian era, as shown here. No longer depicted as a grim skeleton, death is shown instead as a towering woman with wings.

Standing silently amongst the myriad of tombstones, Celtic crosses, and obelisks is the remarkably haunting statue of a little girl frozen in time. The statue is the stone recreation of Grace Sherwood Allen, who died from whooping cough days prior to her fifth birthday.[4] Her delicate curls, the buttons on her tiny shoes, and even the intricate patterns on the lace of her dress are sculpted with stunningly accurate detail. Her eyes glance so lovingly but are also haunting to look at. Her delicate and innocent eyes follow you as you walk through the grounds. She stands alone in the cemetery surrounded safely in a tall glass case, holding a wilted bouquet—an eternal symbol of the brevity of her young life.

Towards the far end of the cemetery is the second immortal child of Forest Hills: often referred to as the Boy in the Boat. The young boy, carved in solid marble, is Louis Ernest Mieusset. Louis is shown seated on a small boat, holding onto a tennis racket. He has one of his legs right outside the boat as if he is about to step into the water below. Like Grace, he is also permanently encased in glass. The life-like details in his hair and large cheeks add to the youthfulness and innocence of his appearance.

The monument had a number of specific attributes added to it by the boy's endlessly grieving mother. Louis' mother had originally added a marble bench with a moveable drawer.[5] She was known as a regular at the cemetery and could be seen cleaning the glass and maintaining her son's grave almost daily. Even when her finances dwindled, she made certain her son's memorial remained as stunning and flawless as when it was created.

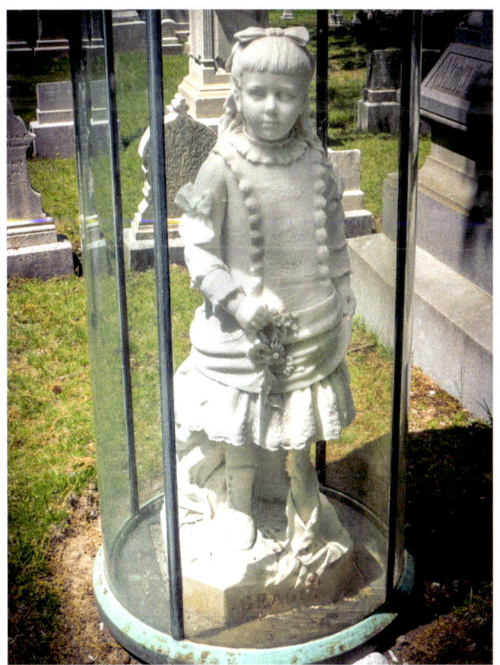

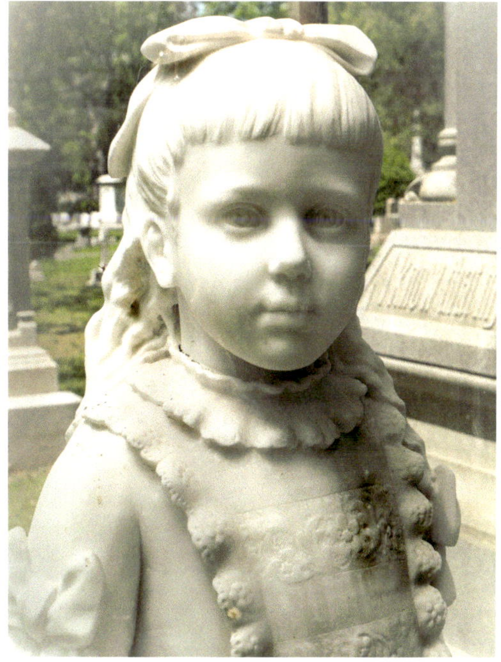

Above left: The stunningly realistic statue of young Grace, forever encased in glass.

Above right: No detail is left unfinished right down to the delicate lace on Grace's dress.

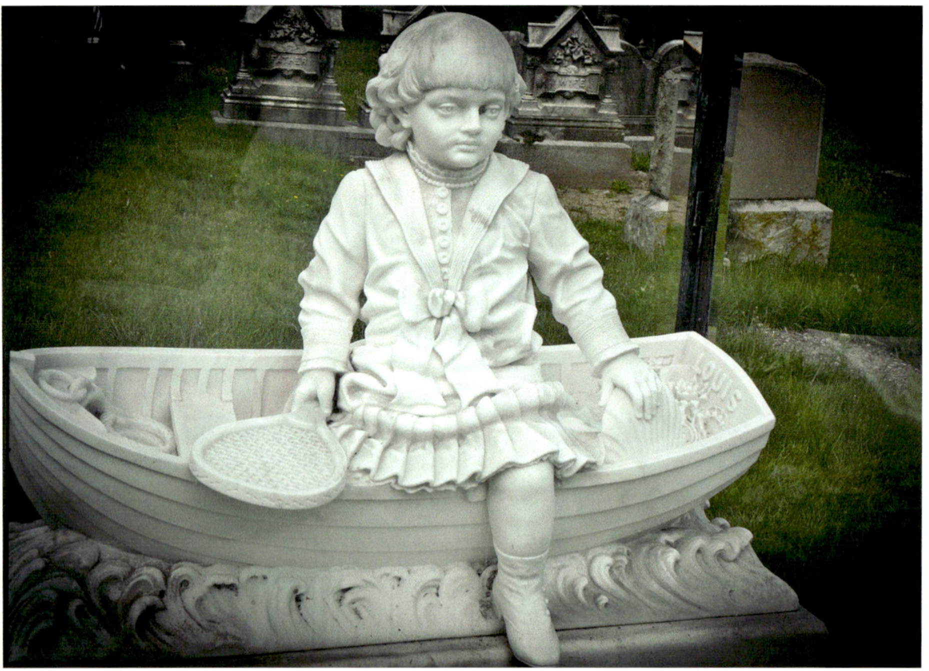

Louis, known famously as "The Boy in The Boat," is a favorite amongst eager taphophiles.

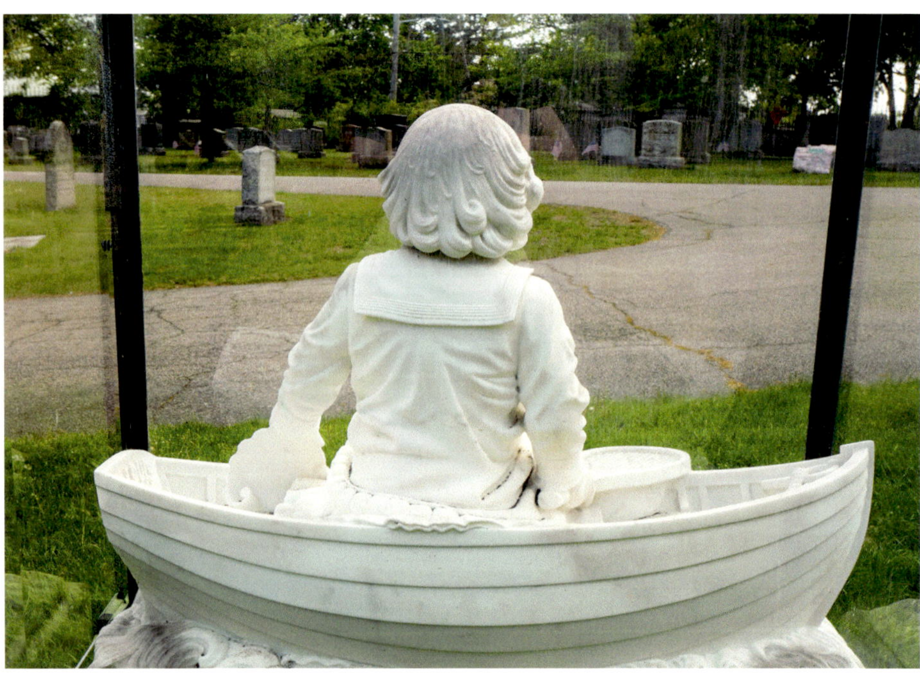

Even though Louis is encased in glass, you are still able to move around unobstructed for a full view of the intricate detail, including his perfect curls.

Rumor has it that the monument depicts the last moment of his life. Stories say that Louis fell from a boat into the water as he attempted to reach his pet rabbit on the nearby shore. The truth is less romantic. According to records, he died from a terrible bout of scarlet fever and a severe kidney infection.[6] Supposedly, even after the death of his mother (whose grave is not specifically marked), fresh flowers are left at the site, anonymously for years after his death.

The glass-encased children are not the only distinctive sculptures to adorn Forest Hills, as the cemetery has a variety of monuments that explore the intimacy of life and death. Some of these monuments are a result of the cemetery's contemporary site-specific art installations located on the Sculpture Path.[7] The trustees of Forest Hills have revived the Victorian tradition of the sculpture garden, incorporating art pieces into the space as lovingly and thoughtfully as the works dedicated to its permanent residents.

One of the most haunting and macabre of these works are the *Resting Benches* created by Danielle Krcmar in collaboration with Lisa Osborn. *Resting Benches*, which are part of more than thirty-five works on the Contemporary Sculpture Path, shows multiple child-size beds recreated in stone.[8] The beds appear to have recently been slept in, evident through the rumpled sheets and indented pillows. Some pillows are tossed on the ground nearby. Empty or vacant furniture, especially chairs and beds, are often a recurring theme. The concept of a bed in this piece, however, has multiple meanings. Krcmar and Osborn's piece is not only a reference to falling asleep, but also to illness, conception, and even the traditional idea of the deathbed.

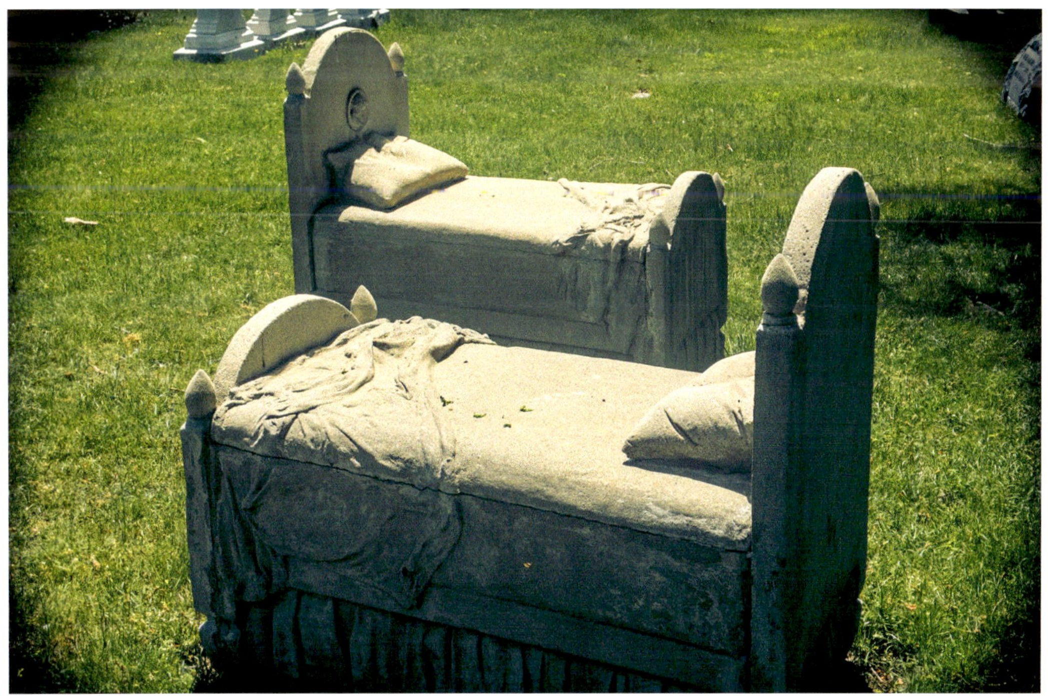

The *Resting Benches* are not dedicated to a particular person but are site-specific art installations.

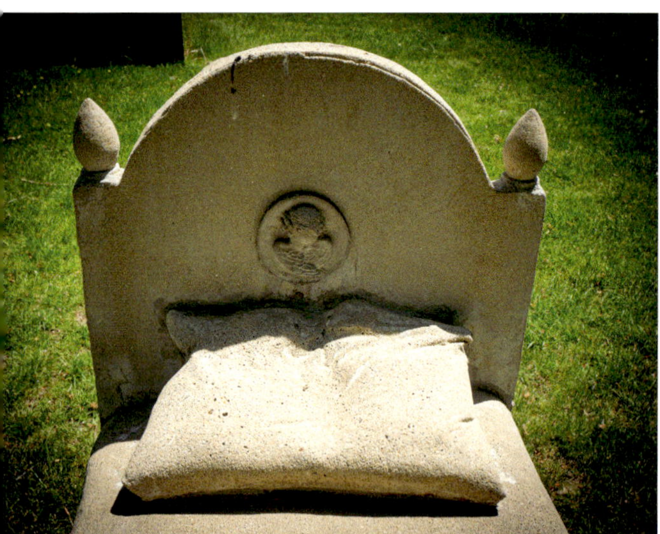

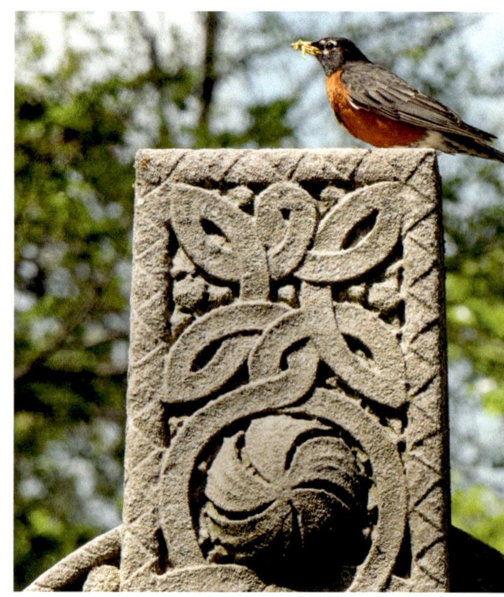

Above left: Beautifully carved, the *Resting Benches* appear as if someone has just woken up, complete with indented pillows.

Above right: A bird catches a quick snack on top of one of many Celtic crosses on the grounds.

Below: In some instances, only the word "mother" or "father" would be found on the gravestones, but that doesn't mean the design is any less elaborate.

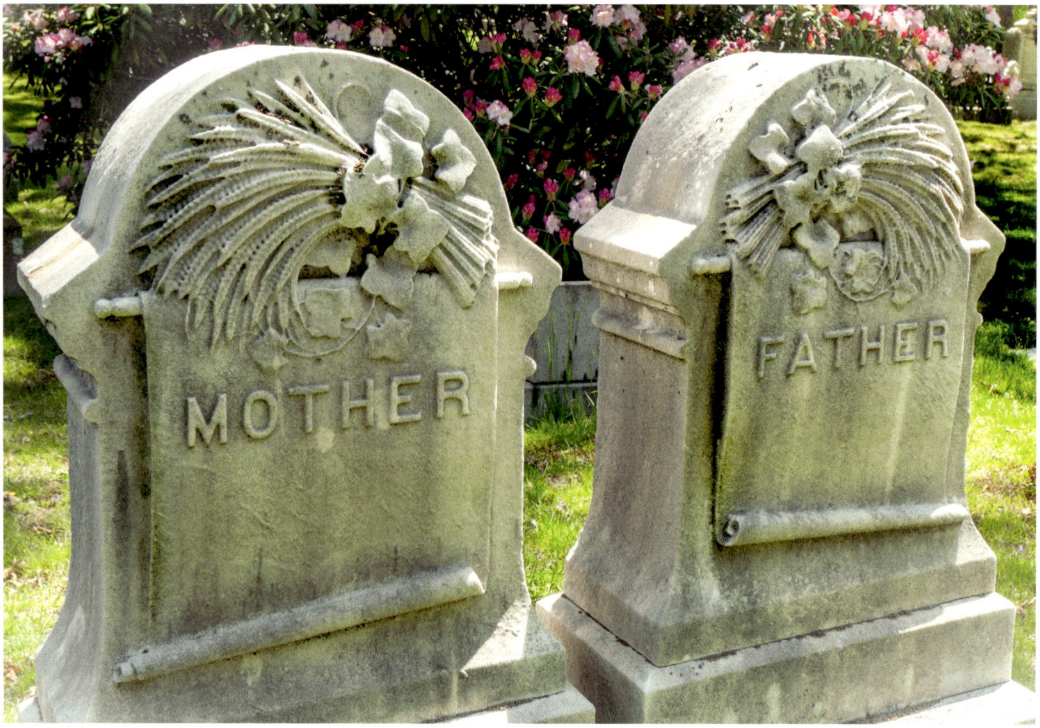

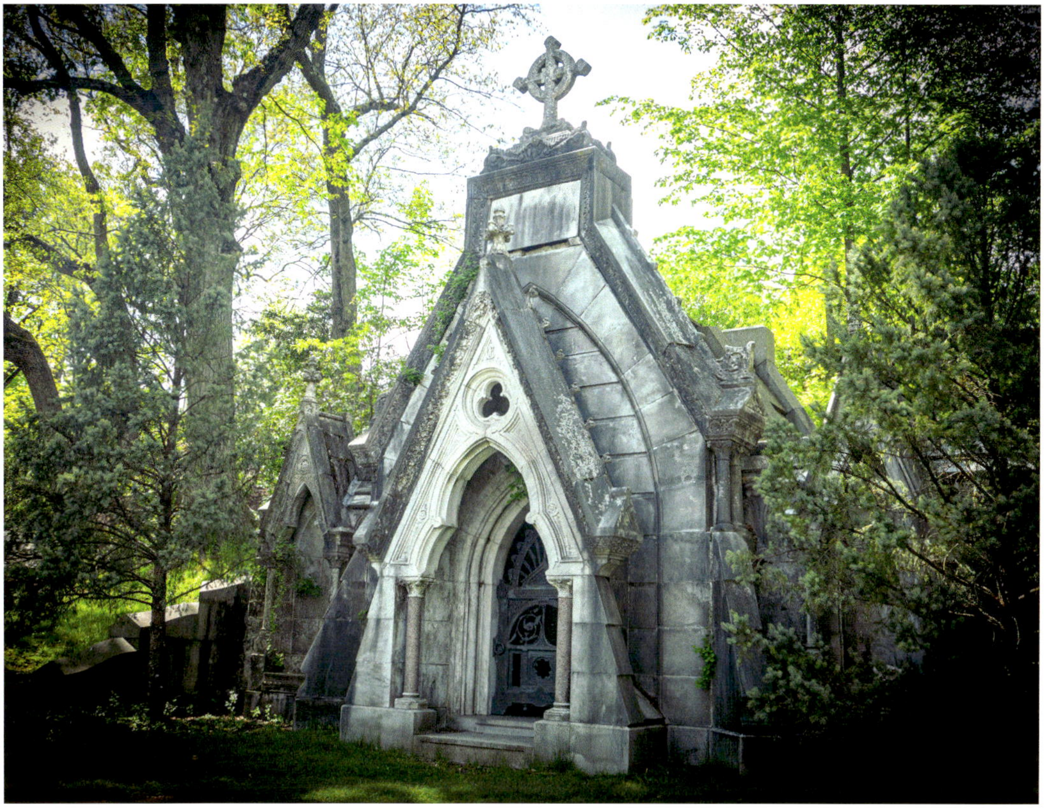

Above: One of the many stunning mausoleums on the grounds; note the beautiful, triangular-shaped Gothic Revival archway.

Right: An angel with a flower garland.

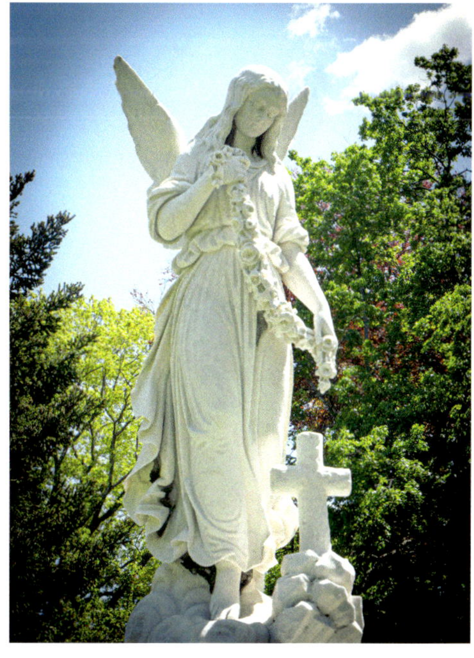

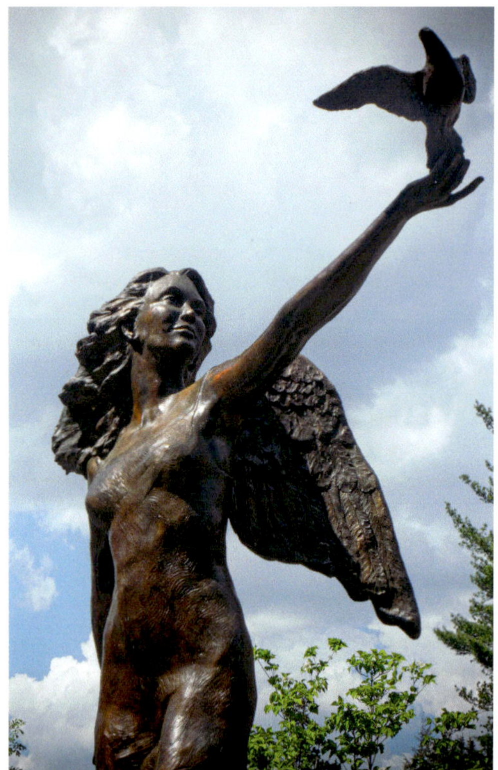

Left: A more modern angel, with her hand outstretched to a bird mid-flight. Birds are often representations of freedom or the Holy Spirit.

Below left: On a beautiful spring day, Forest Hills is filled with bright colored flowers.

Below right: An ascending angel.

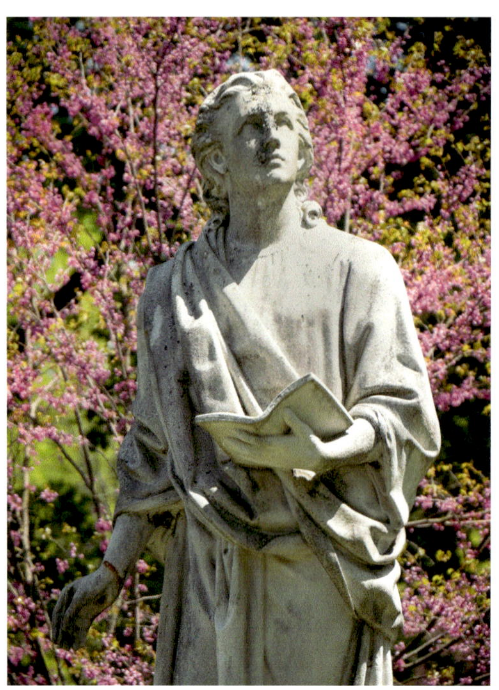

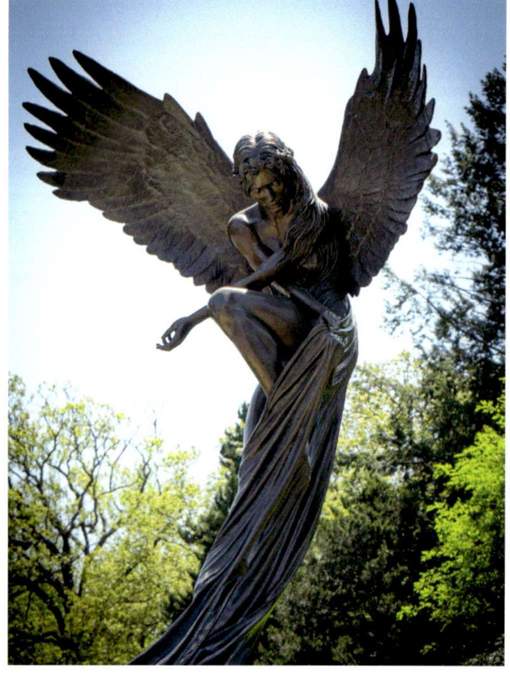

9

St. Michael's Cemetery

A quick run across the road from Forest Hills and past a tall metal gate is the entrance to St. Michael's Cemetery. At first glance, it appears to be like many more modern American Catholic cemeteries, filled with crucifixes and statues of the Virgin Mary with her eyes looking toward the heavens. What makes St. Michael's unforgettable, however, is the hundreds of stone people, each one intricately carved and crafted to perfection.

With its first internment in 1907, Saint Michael's Cemetery was home to the city's large Italian Catholic population.[1] Now a largely non-denominational populace in recent years, it has become non-sectarian, but it stills holds the same provocative appearance and is a stylistic mix of traditional and contemporary.

Many modern cemeteries have etchings or small lockets with photographs as a way to commemorate the deceased. St. Michael's stone replicas of the departed make it a phenomenal location to explore. It is as if they are frozen in time, forever standing guard over the graves of those who had passed. Some, like the many men in their military regalia, are stoic and serious. Husbands and wives are often shown together, as a permanent representation of their commitment to one another. Busts of entire families are seen together on top of tombstones. The attention to detail is incredible, from the way their clothing was textured to the way their hair and faces were sculpted. St. Michael's Cemetery is a beautiful and eerie sight all at once. These spectral stone statues are a permanent reminder of family members long gone and are truly a marvel to behold.

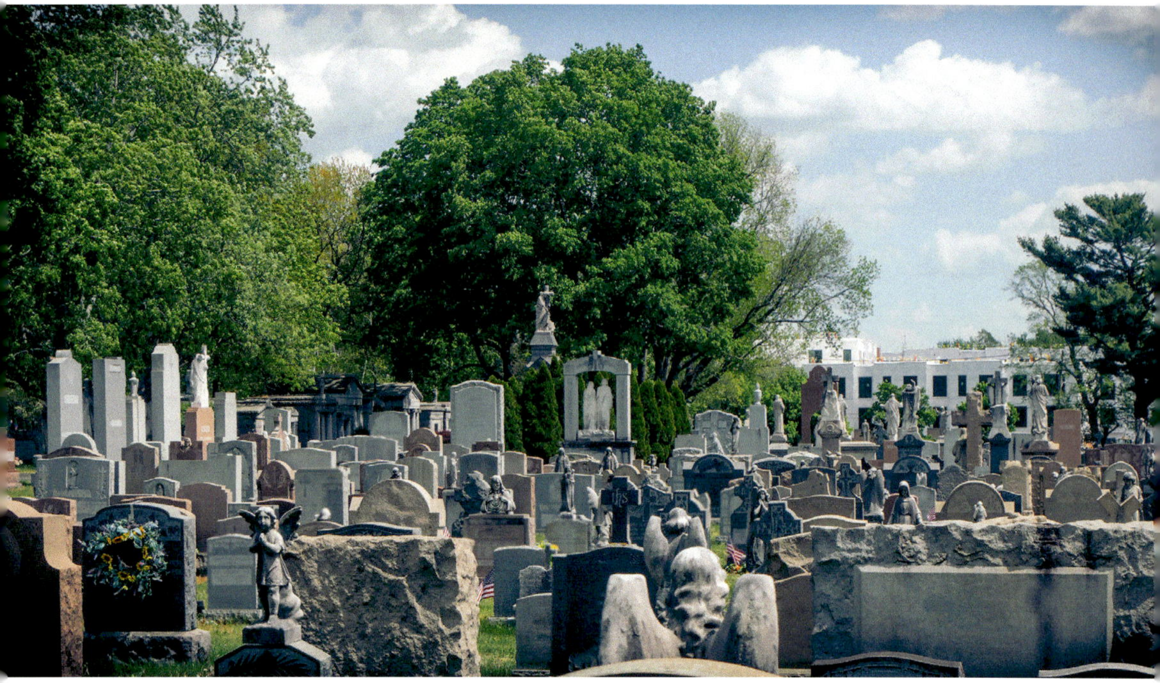

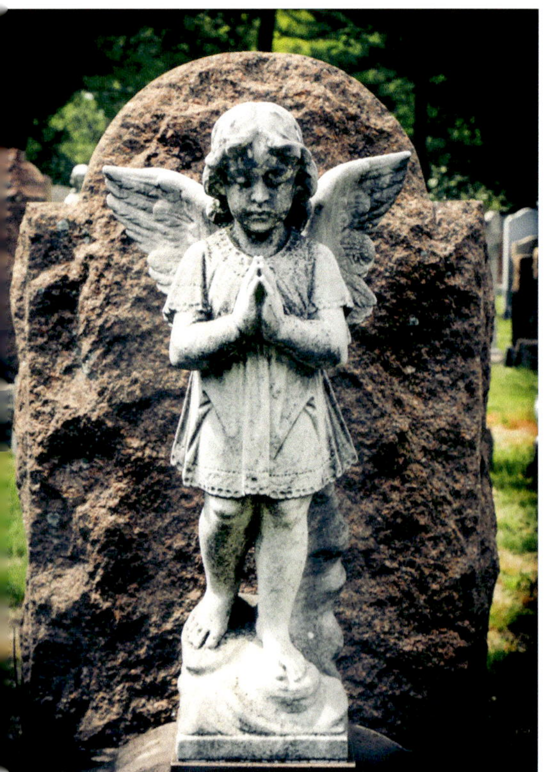

Above: St. Michael's Cemetery is packed with wonderful and unique stones and statues.

Left: St. Michael's is filled with many huge crucifixes and religious statues, but also smaller, demure angels.

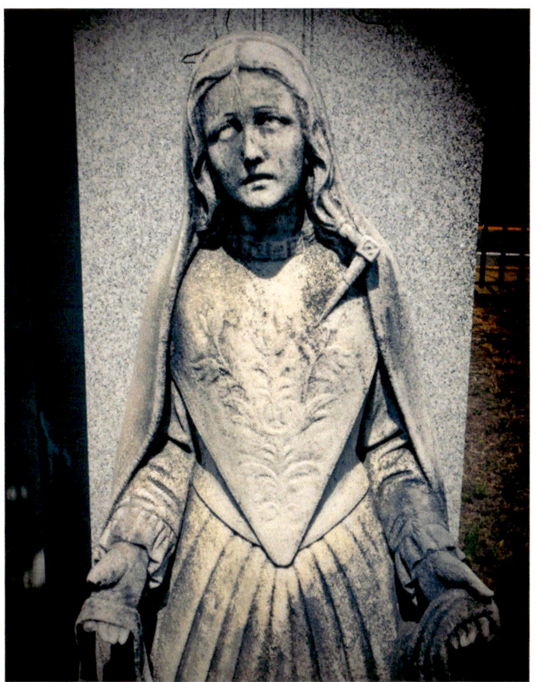

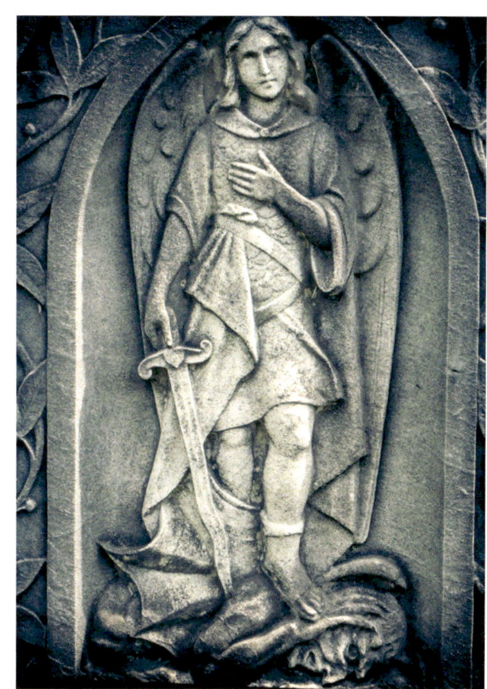

Above left: One of hundreds of saintly statues that are found within St. Michael's Cemetery

Above right: The triumph of good over evil.

Right: A divine angel, complete with radiant halo.

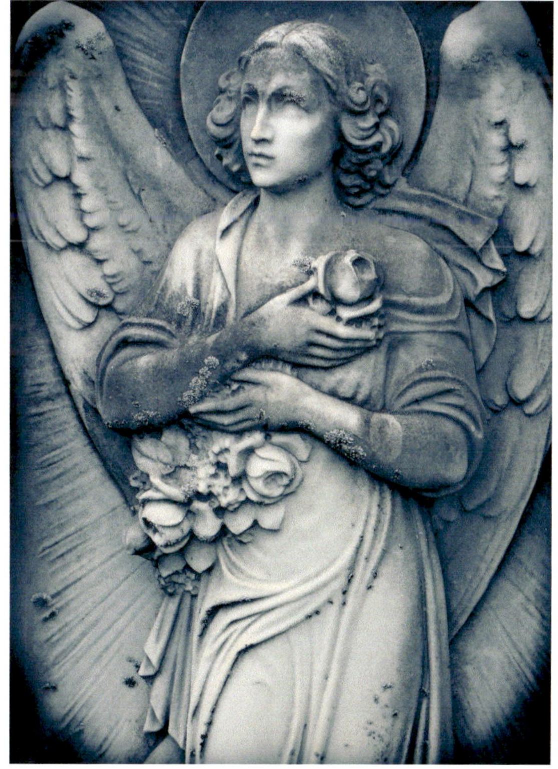

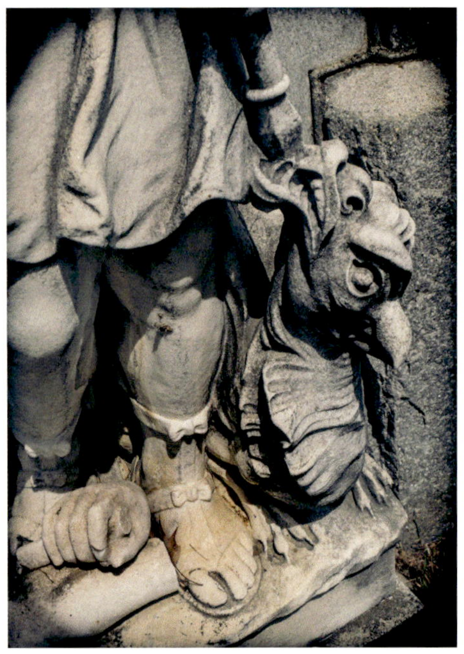

Left: St. George and the Dragon.

Below: St. Michael's has hundreds of statues and busts that are perfect recreations of the deceased. No detail is spared, and they often include stone replicas of jewelry, medals, or, in this case, spectacles.

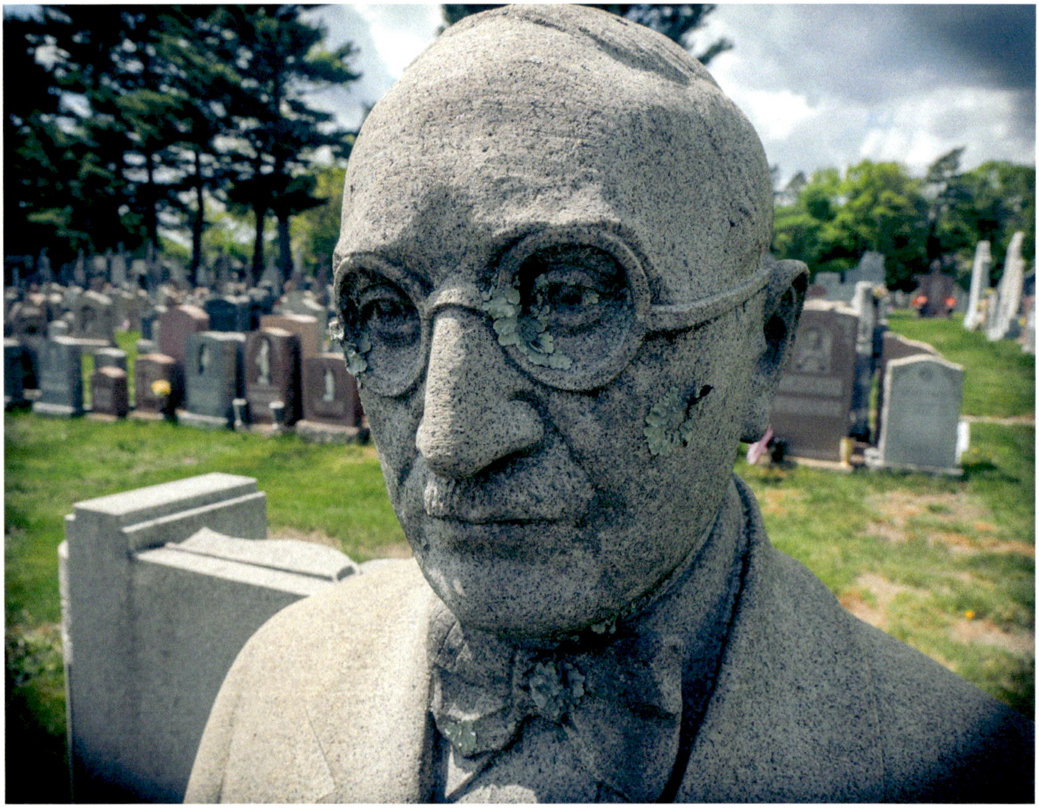

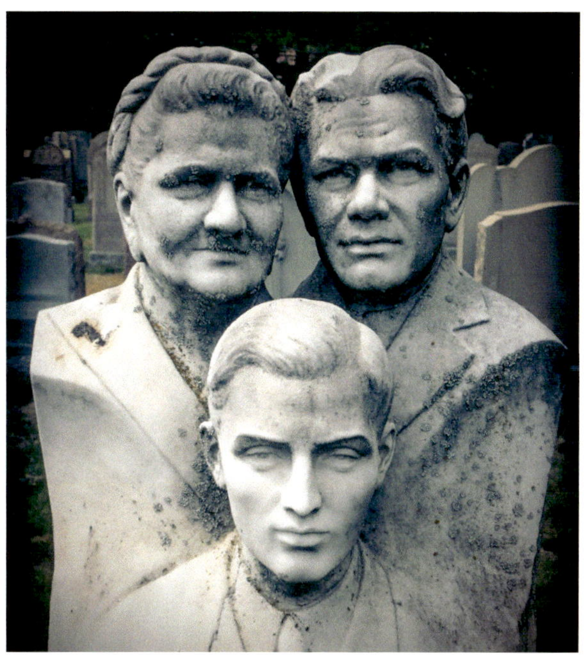

Some monuments recreate stone likenesses of entire families.

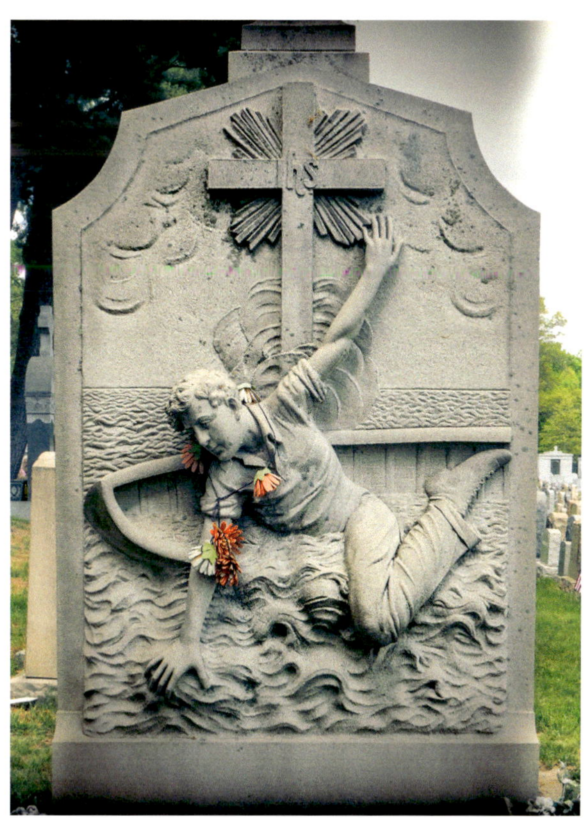

One of the most dynamic monuments in the entire cemetery is this one dedicated to the Cassaro family, which shows a boy falling into a lake.

ENDNOTES

Chapter 1

1. "King's Chapel Burying Ground," accessed June 22, 2023, City of Boston, boston.gov/cemeteries/kings-chapel-burying-ground.
2. Jacobsen, K. R., "New Discovery- Emblemes and Hieroglyphicks: A Quarles Discovery in King's Chapel Burying Ground," *Markers XXXVIII*, (2023): 123–140.
3. *Ibid.*

Chapter 2

1. MacQuarrie, B., "'The Oldest Stone in All of Boston': Visits to Some of the City's Historic Graveyards Are by Appointment Only," accessed July 12, 2023, *The Boston Globe*, July 5, 2022, bostonglobe.com/2022/07/05/metro/leaving-no-stone-untended.
2. *Ibid.*
3. "Sam Danforth," Find A Grave, accessed April 20, 2023, findagrave.com/memorial/117003184/samuel-danforth.

Chapter 3

1. "Grave of John Harvard, in Old Charlestown Burying Ground, Phipps St., Charlestown, Mass.," Digital Commonwealth Massachusetts Collections Online. Accessed August 18, 2023, digitalcommonwealth.org/search/commonwealth:fj236m30n.
2. "The Ingenious Mathematician and Printer," Graphic Arts Collection, Special Collections, Firestone Library, Princeton University, accessed August 18, 2023, graphicarts.princeton.edu/2015/07/28/the-ingenious-mathematician-and-printer/.

Chapter 4

1. "Copp's Hill Burying Ground," The City of Boston, accessed May 26, 2023, boston.gov/cemeteries/copps-hill-burying-ground.
2. Jon, M., *Our Boston*, p. 25 (St. Paul, Minnesota: Voyageur Press 1998).
3. Adams, D., "The Forgotten Legacy of Boston's Historic Black Graveyard," *Boston Magazine*, May 3, 2022, bostonmagazine.com/news/2022/05/03/black-graveyard-legacy/.

Chapter 5

1. "Granary Burying Ground." The City of Boston. Accessed June 2, 2023, boston.gov/cemeteries/granary-burying-ground
2. *Ibid.*
3. Abel, D., (16 May 2011). "Colonial Resting Place Slated for Upgrade," *Boston Globe*, archived from the original on 12 November 2011, retrieved 26 July 2023, web.archive.org/web/20111112184800/http://articles.boston.com/2011-05-16/news/29549185_1_granary-tombs-grave-markers.
4. Woodward, S., "The Story of Smallpox," Massachusetts Medical Society. Accessed May 3, 2023, massmed.org/About/MMS-Leadership/History/The-Story-of-Smallpox-in-Massachusetts/.

Chapter 6

1. History of Central Burying Ground," The City of Boston, accessed April 13, 2023, boston.gov/news/history-central-burying-ground.
2. *Ibid.*
3. *Ibid.*

Chapter 7

1. Linden, B. M., *Silent City on a Hill: Picturesque Landscape of Memory and Boston's Mount Auburn Cemetery*, p. 119 (Amherst, MA: Library of American Landscape History 2007).
2. "Boston Becomes the Antislavery Hub," The Massachusetts Historical Society, accessed May 3, 2023, masshist.org/features/boston-abolitionists/antislavery-hub.
3. Gugliotta, G., "New Estimate Raises Civil War Death Toll." *The New York Times*, 2 Apr. 2012, accessed April 1, 2023, nytimes.com/2012/04/03/science/civil-war-toll-up-by-20-percent-in-new-estimate.html.
4. Wilson, S., *Literary Trail of Greater Boston*, p. 114 (Boston: Houghton Macmillan Press 1998).
5. Bussman, J., "Cemetery Reaches 100,000 Interments," Mount Auburn Cemetery. December 5, 2017, accessed April 5, 2023, mountauburn.org/cemetery-reaches-100000-interments/.
6. "A Death Bed by James Aldritch," Poetry Archive, accessed April 5, 2023, poetry-archive.com/a/a_death_bed.html.

Chapter 8

1. Wilson, S., *Garden Memories: A Guide to Historic Forest Hills*, p. 61 (Boston: Forest Hills Educational Trust 1998).
2. *Ibid.*
3. Marx, W. H., "Boy in the Boat Statue at Forest Hills," Jamaica Plains Historical Society, April 1, 2023, jphs.org/locales/2005/9/30/boy-in-the-boat-statue-at-forest-hills.html.
4. Brown, N. P., "A Verdant Cultural Retreat," *Harvard Magazine*, April 1, 2022, harvardmagazine.com/2022/03/h2-forest-hills-cemetery.
5. Marx, W. H., *op. cit.*
6. "Louis Ernest Mieusset," Find A Grave, accessed April 20, 2023, findagrave.com/memorial/9581530/louis-ernest-mieusset.
7. "Exhibitions and Sculptures," Forest Hills Cemetery, accessed April 10, 2023, foresthillscemetery.com/exhibitions-sculptures/.
8. Brown, N. P., *op. cit.*

Chapter 9

1. "St. Michael Cemetery: Serving the Greater Boston Community for over 100 Years," St. Michael Cemetery, accessed June 30, 2023, stmichaelcemetery.com/history.html.

Bibliography

"A Death Bed by James Aldritch," Poetry Archive, accessed April 5, 2023, poetry-archive.com/a/a_death_bed.html.

"About Us," Forest Hills Cemetery, accessed April 6, 2023, foresthillscemetery.com/about-us/.

Abel, D., "Colonial Resting Place Slated for Upgrade," *Boston Globe*, archived from the original on 12 November 2011, retrieved 26 July 2023, web.archive.org/web/20111112184800/http://articles.boston.com/2011-05-16/news/29549185_1_granary-tombs-grave-markers.

Adams, D., "The Forgotten Legacy of Boston's Historic Black Graveyard," *Boston Magazine*. May 3, 2022, bostonmagazine.com/news/2022/05/03/black-graveyard-legacy/.

Baugher, S., and Richard F. V., and Nassaney, M. S., *The Archaeology of American Cemeteries and Gravemarkers* (Gainsville, Florida: University Press of Florida 2014).

"Boston Becomes the Antislavery Hub," The Massachusetts Historical Society, accessed May 3, 2023, masshist.org/features/boston-abolitionists/antislavery-hub.

Brown, N. P., "A Verdant Cultural Retreat," *Harvard Magazine*, April 1, 2022, harvardmagazine.com/2022/03/h2-forest-hills-cemetery.

Bussman, J., "Cemetery Reaches 100,000 Interments," Mount Auburn Cemetery. December 5, 2017, accessed April 5, 2023, mountauburn.org/cemetery-reaches-100000-interments/.

"Copp's Hill Burying Ground," The City of Boston, accessed May 26, 2023, boston.gov/cemeteries/copps-hill-burying-ground.

Cothran, J. R., *Grave Landscapes: The Nineteenth-Century Rural Cemetery Movement* (Columbia, South Carolina: University of South Carolina Press 2018).

"Exhibitions and Sculptures," Forest Hills Cemetery, accessed April 10, 2023, foresthillscemetery.com/exhibitions-sculptures/.

Faust, D. G., *This Republic of Suffering* (New York, New York: Vintage 2009).

"Granary Burying Ground," The City of Boston, accessed June 2, 2023, boston.gov/cemeteries/granary-burying-ground.

"Granary Burying Ground," The Freedom Trail, accessed August 17, 2023, thefreedomtrail.org/trail-sites/granary-burying-ground.

"Grave of John Harvard, in Old Charlestown Burying Ground, Phipps St., Charlestown, Mass.," Digital Commonwealth Massachusetts Collections Online. Accessed August 18, 2023, digitalcommonwealth.org/search/commonwealth:fj236m30n.

Gugliotta, G., "New Estimate Raises Civil War Death Toll." *The New York Times*, 2 Apr. 2012, accessed April 1, 2023, nytimes.com/2012/04/03/science/civil-war-toll-up-by-20-percent-in-new-estimate.html.

"History of Central Burying Ground," The City of Boston, accessed April 13, 2023, boston.gov/news/history-central-burying-ground.

Jacobsen, K. R., "New Discovery- Emblemes and Hieroglyphicks: A Quarles Discovery in King's Chapel Burying Ground," *Markers XXXVIII*, (2023): 123-140.

Jon, M., *Our Boston*, p. 25 (St. Paul, Minnesota: Voyageur Press 1998).

Keister, D., *Stories in Stone* (Layton Utah: Gibbs Smith 2004).

"King's Chapel Burying Ground," accessed June 22, 2023, City of Boston boston.gov/cemeteries/kings-chapel-burying-ground.

Linden, B. M., *Silent City on a Hill: Picturesque Landscape of Memory and Boston's Mount Auburn Cemetery*, p. 119 (Amherst, MA: Library of American Landscape History 2007).

"Louis Ernest Mieusset," Find A Grave, accessed April 20, 2023, findagrave.com/memorial/9581530/louis-ernest-mieusset.

MacQuarrie, B., "'The Oldest Stone in All of Boston': Visits to Some of the City's Historic Graveyards Are by Appointment Only," accessed July 12, 2023, *The Boston Globe*, July 5, 2022, bostonglobe.com/2022/07/05/metro/leaving-no-stone-untended.

Marcus, J., *Our Boston* (St. Paul, Minnesota: Voyageur Press 1998).

"Martin Milmore Memorial, (sculpture)". *Save Outdoor Sculpture, Massachusetts survey*, 1993, archived from the original on March 4, 2016, retrieved July 21, 2023, siris-artinventories.si.edu/ipac20/ipac.jsp?&profile=all&source=~!siartinventories&uri=full=3100001~!20524~!0#focus.

Marx, W. H., "Boy in the Boat Statue at Forest Hills," Jamaica Plains Historical Society, April 1, 2023, jphs.org/locales/2005/9/30/boy-in-the-boat-statue-at-forest-hills.html.

Meier, A. C., *Grave* (New York, New York: Bloomsbury Publishing USA 2023).

Mitford, J., *The American Way of Death Revisited* (New York, New York: Vintage 2011).

Quarles, F., *The Complete Works in Prose and Verse, of Francis Quarles* (1881), google.com/books/edition/Quarles_Emblems/-UsgAAAAMAAJ?hl=en&sa=X&ved=2ahUKEwiHwMfc7b-BAxX2GFkFHcSxDgQQiKUDegQIDxAD.

"Sam Danforth," Find A Grave, accessed April 20, 2023, findagrave.com/memorial/117003184/samuel-danforth.

"St. Michael Cemetery: Serving the Greater Boston Community for over 100 Years," St. Michael Cemetery, accessed June 30, 2023, stmichaelcemetery.com/history.html.

"The Ingenious Mathematician and Printer," Graphic Arts Collection, Special Collections, Firestone Library, Princeton University, accessed August 18, 2023, graphicarts.princeton.edu/2015/07/28/the-ingenious-mathematician-and-printer/.

"The Story of Smallpox," Massachusetts Medical Society, accessed May 3, 2023, massmed.org/About/MMS-Leadership/History/The-Story-of-Smallpox-in-Massachusetts/.

Wilson, S., *Garden Memories: A Guide to Historic Forest Hills*, p. 61 (Boston: Forest Hills Educational Trust 1998).

Wilson, S., *Literary Trail of Greater Boston*, p. 114 (Boston: Houghton Macmillan Press 1998).

Woodward, S., "The Story of Smallpox," Massachusetts Medical Society. Accessed May 3, 2023, massmed.org/About/MMS-Leadership/History/The-Story-of-Smallpox-in-Massachusetts/.